Alex Weddon, age twelve, with his first shotgun and first rabbit, October, 1966. A lever action Ithaca model supersingle in twenty gauge, modified choke. The black and tan is Badger, a farm rescue and decent rabbit dog.

On the cover:
Mom circling the photographer.

Dad would later crash the motorcycle in a very close call.

photo by Edward R. Weddon, MD. circa 1971

Table of Contents

Introduction

These are all true stories. Just ask my twin sister, Amy. We were delivered into this world by our father, an MD with a general practice in the small town of Stockbridge, Michigan. We completed our family of seven.

Todd, the oldest son and brother Brad trekked overland to a one room schoolhouse almost two miles away to start their formal schooling. Patrice, the oldest sister and third born took me and my twin under her wing and read the Sunday comics to us, taught us multiplication tables and famous authors as part of her pre-school curriculum.The three of us often roamed the eighty acre farm in search of adventure or escape during the 1960s.

Dad was a WWII combat veteran who earned an MD from the University of Michigan. He was grateful to the Army and the G.I. Bill that helped him study and work his way out of a suddenly poor and tough Chicago life. He was a decorated US Army corpsman, and over forty six years his general practice was recognized for excellence by his peers at the county and state level, US senators and governors. Mom, a masters in education, freelance writer and national award winning author never lost her cool. She proved to be a refined counter to our fathers unfettered temper.

After Mom died in 2008 and a heartbroken Dad was nearing his end in 2009, my siblings and I often recalled happier days and many of these stories were retold, mostly unchanged from the polishing of a lifetime of holiday tale-telling.

This collection of stories is the second of three that were serialized in my weekly newspaper, **The Grass Lake Times,** from 2010 and 2011.

The first of the Close Calls on the Farm collection is "Survival of the Funniest" launched as a paperback book on St. Patricks Day, 2013 and the third, scheduled for a 2014 release is "Off to School." Samples of the books table of contents can be seen on page 156.

To the good people that have read my stories and told me of their own close calls, I offer a thank you for the support and material for maybe a fourth book.

Thank you for selecting this book to read. I hope you enjoy "Second Chances" and the other "Close Calls on the Farm" books.

Acknowledgments

I have to thank my parents first of all. It was Mom's idea to purchase the farm just a quarter mile away from their home in Stockbridge, Michigan. She told Dad it was an ideal place to raise a family and they could move into a bigger house and not leave the best neighbors and friends they ever had.

I also have to thank my brothers and sisters. They all saved me from harm or administered first aid at one time or another. Todd, Brad, Patrice and Amy worked smart and hard and by any measure were quite successful with their education and careers and, of course, in raising their children.

Also, my children; Dane, Randi, Mallory and Alaina and wonderful wife, Colleen. Raising four kids gave us a perspective of life that grows more wondrous everyday. They also are witness to the veracity of these stories, having heard them many times and hiked and camped the same trails and woods as their father. Oh how they have grown, yet the land seems the same. Constant in its seasons of change and beauty.

A special thanks to Mary Hashman and sister Patrice for proof reading and to William Latocki for cover design and creative work.

SPRING

Buried by Friends

The end of the school year was mostly a wild and free time when I was in fourth grade. Picnics and field trips added to the fresh air joy of recess. Classes would go outside to read in the shade of elm trees that surrounded the elementary school. It was a welcomed freedom from the wooden seats in nonairconditioned classrooms.

The different classes shared the playground of swing sets, monkey bars and merry-go-rounds. Fourth graders and older were allowed to use the ball diamonds with acres of undulating sand, sawgrass and sandburs for outfields.

Since the outfields were the farthest away from the school, that was where the boys of my class gathered and carried on, out of earshot and sight of the safety patrol. The dirty brown sand was easy to dig out, using giant tin cans borrowed from the school's kitchen garbage. The sand was soon crisscrossed with trenches that grew deeper and longer after every lunch hour recess. One sunny day during our last week of school, we were enjoying the destruction of all the sand works when the time came for my pit to be topped off. Someone suggested that I stand in it and they would fill it in around me.

The sand felt cool against my skin. I held my hands at my sides. "We should leave a vent back here," Jeff, my close friend, pointed out, then added,"If he has gas from being squeezed by the sand, it can blow out."

"Come to think of it, what if he has to go to the bathroom?" Larry asked between lobbing cans of sand around me.

"You know, I have to go now, step aside, boys," said another to a raucous round of guffaws and other biological noises.

Before I could say, "That's the bell, recess is over," I was buried up to my chin, facing away from the school. The retreating gang of schoolmates sounded like laughing hyenas as they ran back to class through big double doors at the end of the elementary school.

Granules of sand blew into my ears. All was quiet. Another gust sent sandburs into my hair and I had to close my eyes. "Well, at least I'm not staring at the sun with my eyelids slit like that poor cowboy on the Rifleman TV show," I told my shadow, trying to be positive and unafraid.

I was going to be in trouble. That was for sure. If my twin sister saw my head out here in the desert, she would dig me out, after an attack of hysteria, I mused. "It is pretty funny. I'll bet there isn't another kid in fourth grade in the whole world that is doing what I'm doing right now," I told myself. One side of my mouth crinkled in pride, breaking free a rivulet of caked facial sand.

A shadow wriggled, and then slithered across my field of vision. I was giving into an overwhelming fear of having a Blue Racer snake wrap around my head when the other side of my brain declared it a mirage.

Panic kept erupting in different flavors. I can't move my arms enough to dig myself out! But I can shift back and forth, so it is only a matter of time, logic countered. Sandbur in my eye! Shut your eyes. Spider on face! Blow it off. What if a cat comes and starts digging a potty? Bark like a dog. What if a dog comes over to go... and so went my mental banter. Only a few minutes must have gone by, but I had been mentally leapfrogging around the world, desert by desert, facing all the scorpions and sidewinders I had seen in National Geographic.

I heard the double doors slam. "At last, someone is coming to help me, probably the janitor coming out for a smoke," I predicted.

"He'll see me and pull me out. He'll have a broom to sweep the sand off my clothes and things will be fine."

Between gentle sand-laden zephyrs of summer wind, I heard footfalls crunching on the dried grass of the playground. "Someone is coming, I'm sure of it," I thought. "Why don't they say something?"

"When your teacher told me, I had to come out here to see it myself. Mr. Weddon...." I couldn't hear the rest of the welcome, the voice of our school's principal registered into my mind's hotel panic for a long stay.

"I'll never make fifth grade," I blubbered to myself. "She's gonna tell Mom and Dad and that will be it. Grounded for the summer. Oh! I can be so stupid sometimes. Some friends." On and on tumbled the voice of my conscience over Miss P's muffled voice in the background.

A shadow drew over me as she stepped near. "Mister Alex, just what are we going to do with you? Your teacher didn't know where you were. She thought you might be on the school's roof again, or in the basement tunnels, but out here? Really!" She crossed her arms, making her shadow look like the silhouette of an attacking Pterodactyl. "Your teacher is trying to teach her class. But just look, they are all

12

lined up at the window looking at a dirty little head in the sand and their principal. What kind of boy lets his friends do this to him? Hmmmm?"

She had laid out so many arguments I didn't know where to start. Maybe I could cry and she'd give in. I couldn't decide which brilliant plan would save me from this fix.

"I see you almost have your arms free. Here, let me help." And with that, she helped me dig out one arm at a time. It didn't take long and we were walking back to the school. I was shaking sand out of my clothes and hair with every step. We pushed through the double doors and down the hallway to my class.

My teacher will be mad, the class will laugh at me, but I'm not in too much trouble, I thought. By my next step, hope vanished. The principal held my arm and escorted me right past my classroom door and down the long hall to her office.

I stayed in her office in penitent silence until the school day ended and it was time to ride the bus home. She looked over her black framed reading glasses, their silver chain draped down and back around her neck, "You're excused to go," She wagged a boney finger for emphasis. "But come back to this office first thing in the morning."

The consensus on the school bus was that a gigantic punishment was waiting for me. It was suggested that I flee to Canada. A plan for me to come down with a disease gained traction. Diarrhea and it's colorful variations was popular and discussed in great juvenile detail. Rabies gained favor until someone reminded me it was always fatal. In those days, any and all facts of life could be learned on a school bus, no need to "Google it."

The next morning, I checked in and served my time in her office chair. I remember the sticky heat and her wall clock ticking. It wasn't my first stretch of principal-office time, but it was the last for that school year.

Swinging Past Cars

Swinging on a rope over water and dropping and splashing into a lake is exhilarating. Swinging on a rope into the flow of traffic is equally fun and also affords the opportunity of sharing the adrenaline rush with an unsuspecting driver.

The road in front of my childhood farmhouse cut through an embankment that rose about five feet above the pavement. Stretching skyward from the crest was an ancient and dying elm tree. The monarch harbored two tree houses and a magnificent rope swing. The tree houses were nothing more than decks made of old barn siding with a short railing to keep us from rolling off.

To access the tree top patios, we would climb ten feet up a nearby sapling and then onto the elm's first overhanging branch, shinny along it toward the main trunk and under the trap door.

The platform was built where a few branches spread like outstretched arms from the main trunk. One ran directly over the embankment, parallel to the road. This was the ideal spot to hang a swing.

Richie, our neighbor and at fifteen, the oldest, positioned himself on the limb, as big around as a sheep and over twenty feet up. We tossed him a length of baler twine and tied our end to the rope. This was the biggest rope I had ever seen in my thirteen years. It was at least two inches thick and plenty long enough, donated to the cause by Brian, another of the neighborhood gang and my age. We knotted a loop in one end and Richie hand-hauled it up. He then pulled the other end through the loop and dropped it to us. We double knotted the end for a sizeable seat.

The fun went something like this. Grab the swing a couple of feet above the knot, run from the tree trunk and then jump away from the bank while pulling yourself up and onto the seat. Our little bodies were flinging away, coming to a pause and then a big pendulum swing back, soaring over the road and well past the trunk to a landing. The swing arc was at least forty-five feet and the flight time was awesome.

It just so happened one mid-spring day that Richie's older brother, Denny, was driving past the tree in the family station wagon. Richie timed his swing so that he was able to look in the passenger side of the cruising car and say, "Hey Denny, where ya going?" The car's brake lights shot on. He stopped and backed up. "Let me try that!" demanded Denny.

It was a thrilling afternoon for us and most of the drivers that caught glimpses of children flying past them from out of the shadows. Like most major innovations, it was misunderstood and the authorities put a stop to our swinging past cars within the week. Only after lengthy counter arguments and the resolution of a few trivial safety issues were we allowed back across the road to fly with the sparrows.

A year or so later, Dutch elm disease toppled the old tree. I recycled the trap door into another tree fort. Brian came and retrieved his hawser. My sisters and I watched from a shady perch in a nearby tree as he dragged it across the fields to his farm. It looked like he was being stalked by a thirty-foot python.

April Fools' Day Classics

For our conniving family unit, it was customary to play tricks or harmless pranks on unsuspecting friends on April Fool's Day. I would like to outline a couple of pranks that worked pretty well for me in my long-ago childhood.

The first is the old bed sheet-in-a-pancake trick, (which is good to foist upon the parents). The night before, offer to make your mom and dad breakfast the next morning. Forget about the coffee. When you pull this one off, they will be wide awake and may even be getting some needed exercise by chasing you around the breakfast table.

Grab a box of Jiffy Mix pancake mix (made in nearby Chelsea), and get an old rag. My siblings and I used retired cloth diapers, a dwindling resource in today's world. Old bed sheets are a good plan B, so pull one off the bed and go to work cutting five to ten squares about two inches on a side. Heat and grease the skillet, pour in the pancake mix to make three to four inch diameter hotcakes and just as bubbles form on the top, drape in your cut-up bed sheet, add some batter and flip. The fresh batter should spread evenly over the sheet square as it fries.

Keep the parents occupied by asking them to read this book to you (it may be wise to pull the bookmark from this page first) and when the pancakes are done, serve them up with some maple syrup and butter.

When you see the tears of appreciation in your mom's eyes, don't have second thoughts about pulling off this joke. Remember, she would get all leaky-eyed if you were only serving up a glass of water, so stay on task and serve the hotcakes piping hot.

Then the fun begins. Mom will politely try to overlook the difficulty in cutting up a piece to eat. She will be looking at you lovingly and praising herself for raising such wonderful children. Dad will be looking at his food and checking out the serving plate, judging how many he can eat before being compelled by Mom to share with the children.

Oh, the laughs you will get from almost everyone in the room when those pancakes are mangled to look like mashed potatoes. This might be a good time to go back into the kitchen and out the back door, as dad will then realize what is up and allow a small amount of rage to boil over.

This should make for an interesting day or week, depending on your family's level of anger management.

The second April Fools' joke has to do with your brothers or sisters. I did this and my eleven-year-old twin sister almost required defibrillation.

Using old kite string (fishing line may work, if it can hold a knot) tie one end to a few items in the victim's bedroom and run the line along the baseboard (usually hard to see with all the clothes lying around) and out the door a few feet.

When the sibling is sleeping, start pulling on the strings one at a time at strategic intervals (between screams of terror, for example). Having one tied to a rocking chair is good; tying up the corner of the victim's pillow is even better. Continue pulling your assortment of strings, being careful to allow some clearance from the doorway, as it is common for a body to come rocketing out after the pillow string is pulled. You may want to plant the extra, unused string in another sibling's room. Call it insurance.

Mail Order Chicken Dinner

Did you know that the U.S. Postal Service still delivers chicks in the mail? Mom was able to take advantage of this fine service years ago when I was about eleven years old. She had made her daily run to the post office in town, arriving just before five o'clock closing to mail her correspondence with a number of newspapers. We were intrigued by a cheep cheep cheep behind the counter.

As I stood at her side, the conversation went something like this: "Someone ordered these chicks," the postmaster said, "And hasn't been in to pick them up." We have to get rid of them."

"Oh my, what a shame." Mom clucked "Maybe I could use them," Mom clucked. "How much do you need for them?"

As with most situations Mom found herself in, she would listen carefully for opportunity knocking. She could always concoct a plan to make the best of it. This was no exception. She gave the man two dollars and left the post office with 200 baby chickens. By the time she returned to our farm, she had hatched a plan.

She called a neighboring farm wife and swapped half the fluffy yellow chicks for a watering can and advice as to how to raise and harvest the future Sunday dinners. She lodged the little cheepers in the basement, we sheltered them in the cardboard box our new TV came in with a heat lamp over it. Being in the newspaper business, Mom had plenty of material to line the box, and the chicks made themselves right at home. My older sister, Patrice, my twin sister, Amy and I marveled at the little critters and were happy to give them chick feed. My older brothers, Todd and Brad, were exempt from chicken chores, as they had livestock of their own to tend.

They chicks cheeped constantly and produced, according to Mom, "lovely fertilizer for the garden." It seemed that for every pound of feed we gave them, we received two pounds of fertilizer in return.

My beagle sat at the head of the basement steps, head cocked, waiting for a chance to settle things. Our cats pricked their ears forward and licked their chops by the main floor heat registers directly over the little flock.

During breakfast we heard cheeping. Coming in from the school bus, we heard cheeping, watching our new color TV, we heard cheeping, and going to bed we heard cheeping.

After a week, it became apparent the chicks must be relocated. It was decided for the sake of family harmony to put them in the fenced-in old chicken coop/dog house, and that meant Dad's bird dogs had to go back on chains.

The yellow poultry puff balls turned into gangly white birds that soon flew the coop. They ran all over the yard and farm, often motivated into high gear by Dad's Brittanys lunging to the end of their chains, bug-eyed and gasping. This contributed to the birds laying eggs in the most unlikely places. We found eggs or empty shells in the driveway, on the porch and oddly, more than a few near the chained dogs. Laid in a hurry to assist in take off perhaps? I could only guess.

In late June, Mom planned to welcome summer vacation with an old-fashioned chicken harvest. She partially filled a forty gallon horse trough with water, and set it over hot coals to boil. The freshly murdered birds would be dipped and blanched in the scalding water to loosen feathers, then plucked, gutted, cooled and wrapped for the freezer.

To start the process, we gathered in the front yard under the spreading limbs of a Catalpa tree. Mom assigned twelve gauge shotguns to my brothers and, for safety reasons, gave my twin and me an axe. "Who will collect the most birds?" she asked.

A hen peacefully strutted in front of the blue metal garage door. Kabang! Feathers flew and the door shuddered, blue paint chips fluttered. Schlick-catick, Brad racked in another round and crowed, "There's one for ya, Ma."

Patrice loped along, sheparding them into a corner for easier collection, or she picked up expired birds. Amy snagged her first bird by a wing. She put one hand on its head, the other on both legs and stretched the bird's neck over a stump in front of me. Whack! Off came the head and some of the breast. I should have warmed up to sharpen my aim, but time was a wastin'.

Amy recoiled in horror. The hen's wings flapped as it ran zig-zagging across the yard, blood gushing in spurts. BLAM, the bird rolled and lay still, white feathers drifting in the silence. "That doesn't count for you!" I protested to Todd. Amy fetched another.

If chaos had a plural, this was it. With all the noise and smoke, the livestock ran to the far side of the pasture. The birds were in a panic, the dogs were barking, bolting to the end of their chains and flipping over. The smell was awful. Steaming wet chickens smell worse than wet goats. We put up about sixty birds that bloody day. Of course, my brothers harvested the most.

Toward evening, ten chickens materialized. Taking pity on the poor birds, Patrice had given sanctuary to her captures in her tack box, and when all was clear, released them.

During our next chicken dinner, conversations around the table would be interrupted by the occasional pit-tinks of lead shot spit onto a plate to accentuate one claim or another. And that's why, to this day, I always eat chicken carefully. I don't want to break a tooth.

Bozo, loyal farm dog. He adopted the Weddon family the day they were searching for a runaway Brittany spaniel. He approached them from under the front porch of an abandoned home and won their hearts.

Dogs in Danger

Our dogs didn't have it easy on the farm. Dad had his bird dogs, and they were kept on chains or safely in a pen. The other dogs ran loose around the farm but did have their own doghouse. This off-kilter assortment of wood and a roof wasn't pretty, but it served its purpose of disguising the small sinkhole of our well, just a step or two from our back door.

Our fresh water came from a 270-foot length of well pipe that went down through gravel, salt water and sand before reaching fresh, iron-rich water. After putting the doghouse over it, my sisters and I noticed that it was slowly listing into the ever growing pit.

The off kilter angle of the doghouse was of some concern to us. "There is no way that doghouse will fall down the well," Dad told us outright. But it still continued to sink.

We had all seen TV Westerns where a cowboy gets caught in quicksand and starts sinking. "Could that happen to us?" my sisters and I thought out loud as we circled and inspected the tilting doghouse. "They sank in quicksand because they wriggled around so much. You have to fall on your back to spread out your weight and work to the edge to be safe," Dad instructed. It was reassuring to know that he always had solutions to dangerous situations.

We used heavy oak slabs for the doghouse floor/well cover. We made sure the dogs wouldn't dig under the boards. If they were successful in escaping summer's heat beneath the slabs, they could end up somewhere near the center of the earth. And we all knew how hot that was.

After a few years, and a few more spontaneous renovations, the doghouse was moved and the entrance to the farmhouse was spruced up. A small cement porch and a step were poured. Within two years, the porch was tilting away from the house towards the hungry sink-hole.

The dogs made themselves useful by barking at and chasing cars, peeing on visitors' cars and jumping on and scratching cars. Getting hit by cars was a fate they all shared. It was the one great lesson. Survivors were then considered trained and welcomed into the family pack.

Getting run over was a hazard for the feral canines. A schoolmate of my older teenage sister backed over my black and white beagle with her family's station wagon. Snoopy survived another seventeen years with a paralyzed right rear leg, barely able to earn his keep. We were companions and spent many days together, me trying to teach him to retrieve, or to come when called.

Snoopy was just smart enough to be sneaky. I adjusted to his three-legged gait, and he indifferently tolerated the fact that I couldn't smell anything. When on a track, he would stop and look at me to make sure I knew what he was doing. Otherwise he would disappear, ending up back at home.

One fine spring day the beagle was hopping along with me across a neighboring farm's open field when a small herd of pigs foraging behind a new electric fence started moving away from us, attracting Snoopy's interest. These animals were new to him and demanded immediate attention. Off he ran. He splashed into muddy spring run-off water and ducked under the wire, almost.

In a burst of bark he turned on his back and snapped at the electrified wire. With the next jolt, his teeth clenched onto the wire. Another electrifying yelp. He clamped down harder.

I was running as fast as I could to the poor pup. It seemed he was crying out with every third leap I took. I couldn't think what to do. He was trapped in the middle of a puddle, the wire wedged like dental floss between his teeth.

The electric fence amperage for hogs is much higher than the shocking power used for sheep or horses. My loyal friend was conducting it all with every pulse. As I arrived, he broke free and shot by me like a black and white cannon ball. Ol' Snoops bolted for half a mile on what looked like four good legs to me.

Bozo, a liver and white Springer spaniel that had adopted us, had more than one close call on the farm with Dad. One sunny May day the dog was trotting along a lane ahead of Dad and me. We were on our Ford Powermaster tractor, returning a borrowed disk harrow or disk to a neighbor's farm. The implement had four axles of sharpened steel, dinner plate-like disks that sliced into plowed soil to prepare it for planting. When being pulled from barnyard to field, the disks were raised off the ground, but with this one, the clearance was only one or two inches. We couldn't figure out how to raise it anymore than that. I was riding along with Dad, leaning up against a rear wheel fender, looking back to see if the disk hit any stones or roots as we pulled into the farmer's yard.

An average sized black dog erupted from under a corncrib and ambushed the intruding Bozo. The impact drove the two under the leading right wheel. The front of the tractor rose and fell over the tangled fighters.

The black dog stopped snarling and jumped off of Bozo, who twisted and was then under the rear tractor wheel. I was directly above his knotted body as we went over his ribcage. Dad slammed a boot down on the clutch, but not the brake.

The Ford lurched ahead as the big wheel rolled downhill off the dog. Now the disk was turning onto Bozo. My eyes were fixed on the soil scoured plates as they closed on the dog. The brakes squealed and the tractor stopped, the disc jolted against the drawbar and halted, the blades an inch or so from his spine.

Bozo wobbled to all fours, shook and trotted back to the front of the tractor. The neighbor's dog, considering the crushing weight of the tractor as that of the intruder, now gave Bozo plenty of distance and respect. That didn't go unnoticed by Bozo. He trotted proudly ahead of us after we unhitched the disk and headed for home. It had turned out to be a good day for the dog, even after two close calls on the farm.

First Cutting

Putting up hay doesn't take as many hands today as it did on our farm in the 1960s. Big round bales of over eight hundred pounds have replaced the sixty to eighty pound twine-bound bales of yore. Round or small bales, the first cutting is still the most lush and desirous.

As spring warmed our farm with sun filled days our alfalfa and timothy fields grew and flowered. The lush crop awaited the first cutting, nodding with every breeze in various greens and purples. When Dad judged the crop as ripe, he began preparations for harvest. To start the work, he pulled on a fresh pair of white goatskinned gloves and fired up the tractor. He backed the Ford into the pole barn and attached the sickle bar hay mower to his tractor's PTO (power take off) three-point hitch. The cutting bar was a flattened ribbon of steel, about five inches wide and eight feet long. It was basically a saw with eight feet of Tyrannosaurus Rex sized teeth, a wicked and dangerous piece of equipment. The standing hay would topple over the ratcheting blade in cascading waves.

Unfortunately, the first mowing coincided with nesting season for ground birds, especially pheasants. Try as he could to avoid it, Dad would mow over a nest with the hen protecting her clutch and holding her ground unto death. Because of this, Dad rode the tractor alone. It was customary for at least one of us to ride along with him when plowing or cultivating or raking hay, but he had to concentrate on the mower blade. He knew how quickly it could cut and kill.

Bozo, our liver and white Springer spaniel almost lost both his back legs to the mower. The birds that ran had the dog bounding through the field and the mower caught him from behind. Dad stopped but not before the blade gnashed Bozo's back legs to the bone.

That first cutting had to wait until Dad and dog returned from emergency surgery at the veterinary clinic at Michigan State University. Bozo recovered completely and never showed any side effects of the maiming. He did, however, stay clear of running mowers after that, giving them long lugubrious looks.

The cut field would dry for a day in the early spring sun and fill the farm with a wonderful aroma. The forage had to be raked into long, fat rows for the hungry baler.

Sometimes I would ride on the rake, watching the hypnotic rotations of the tines, chains and gears below me, holding on with both hands in the bumpy field.

Soon a parade of equipment would enter the field. Leading would be the tractor, followed by the hay baler with the flatbed wagon attached. The old McCormick baler motor had to be hand cranked to fire up and that was always a job for the strong arms of Dad or my older brothers. The motor would cough, then hit, spinning the handle out of their hands and flying erratically. We always gave the person cranking plenty of space. Both brothers have scars on their arms from the brass business end of that hand crank.

Brad, the second oldest, would drive the tractor. Apparently he was allergic to hay and had to be up front in the sweet, clear air. He wore a white straw cowboy hat with a red bandanna and rarely looked back to us on the wagon, but watched the baler gobble the endless windrow of dried hay and occasional crimped flat rabbit or pheasant. The tractors exhaust, the balers exhaust and the flying chaff and dust were for the two farmhands on the wagon. Oldest brother Todd stood on the wagon and snagged oncoming bales with a hay hook. In a smooth motion he lifted the bale, bringing up his knee to boost the bale into the air. Just at the point between going up and coming down, he would direct the bale and toss it into place. A sister would lean into the bale to set it square, and then turn away from the following cloud of dust and chaff. After thousands of bales over his high school years, Todd used the same motions to stack opponents when playing varsity football, and mostly without the knee lift.

When the wagon had so many bales on it that Todd had to hop off, Brad would stop.

One of us would hitch the full wagon to a second tractor. With a cough and a roar the the old tractor pulled us to the barn through cool, fresh air. Brad would continue on, the baler excreting bales from a cloud of dust and chaff onto the field.

"Like crap through a goose!" Todd sagely observed to those riding the wagon with him on top of the bouncing stacked bales.

One memorable first cutting, I was in the barn, waiting to unload a wagon. Our neighboring farmer, Dick Price was over to help. He and his brothers operated Price Brothers Auctioneering. I was always eager to hear his "fast talk" as I called it. I sang him a ballad I wrote called Broken Haystack. One refrain went "The bales turned over and killed poor Rover...broken haystack." Dick nodded and grinned his approval. A short time later, Dick had a big selling 45 rpm record with his version of The Auctioneer Song, the b-side had Stagger Lee on it, but no Broken Haystack.

It was later in the afternoon and the barn was just getting hotter and hotter. After an empty wagon pulled out of the barn, Dick reached into a wet canvas pouch for a can of beer. He opened it with a "church key" opener. I was only about 14, but that beer was my first and I will never forget how it cut the dust. I wasn't so sure about the taste. My next long drink came from the water tank hose.

By the end of the day, our hair was thick with chaff and our clothes sweat soaked and crusty. Salt rings formed around our cotton shirt armpits and crept out along the bills of our baseball caps. The back of our necks glowed red from sunburn.

When the last wagon of the day was unloaded, everyone flopped on for a ride to the north end of the farm and its shady woods and cool lake water. We'd change into our swim suits in the tar papered barn wood shack near the lake. Then off the end of the dock we flew into ten feet of spring-fed glory.

Moods were uplifted and soon cannon balls and jack-knifes became the order of the fading day.

The fresh water apparently had a miraculous effect on Brad's allergies because he recovered enough to go on a date that night. Sadly, his allergies returned with the second cutting.

The Third Vote

Understandably, when considering the pros and cons of a temptation, the general population does not include a third vote when wavering between right and wrong. As a twin, I had an extra advocate that often influenced my choices, for better or worse.

I was born weighing in at over eight pounds, a decent sized boy, and my sister slipped into this world behind me at just over five pounds. The two of us rounded out the kid count at five in our family of seven. Mom and Dad had been raising kids for ten years when we came along and they had a practiced parenting skill set that encouraged learning by experience. Following the rare occasions when parental control did step in to spare limb or skin, an after action report would find a lesson in the retelling of the close call in hopes of preventing a recurrence.

As twins, Amy and I shared classrooms in elementary school and sometimes sat together on the bus. Following special speech classes in second and third grades, we gave up on our own language catching on.

During my formative years in the early grades, Amy was the third voice in my head, and often cast the deciding vote when mischief and good judgement were locked in a struggle to prevail.

Together we endured the same classrooms until we were let loose in the halls of our middle school, me to wood shop and her to home economics.

At the age of four we had a string of bad judgements that have over the years turned into a great appreciation of our parents capability to deal with emergencies. The series of close calls began when opportunity met curiosity. One hot and dry August day, Amy and I were walking up our gravel driveway toward the family car and decided to smell some gas. I liked the smell of gas, it was before the time of stinky unleaded fuel and seasonal additives.

Our fertile four-year-old brains guessed there was an unlimited source of gas in there and all we had to do was open the little door and smell. I unscrewed the nose high gas cap and looked across the opening at Amy. After a moment we decided to crawl up on the wide trunk and just lean over for another whiff or two. Mom happened by and pulled me off the trunk with Amy. I don't remember the rest of the day, but we never did it again.

A second close call unfolded later that year when the two of us escalated fun to trouble. The momentum towards disaster began when we were picking up kernels of corn off the dirt floor of the garage/carriage house. We had been attracted to the flock of sparrows noisly fighting over the spilled grain and went to investigate. Amy picked up a kernel with each hand and looked at me. I had some in one hand and put them in my mouth and pushed them out with my tongue. Amy and I laughed and it was her turn. She put one piece of corn up her nose. That was so funny she put the other kernel up her vacant nostril. By then I had picked up more corn and was shoving them in my ears. Before long we had stuffed all our exposed orifices with corn. We were laughing so hard we wobbled.

We stopped giggling and shifted our focus to reclaiming the planted corn. Not having any experience in digging out hard corn, we were not very good at it and soon were crying.

The extractions required equipment we didn't have on the farm and our condition was declared beyond domestic help. We had to go to Dad's medical office. When any of us had to go there, it meant all efforts had failed and we had to interrupt Dad in his office. All of my siblings were stitched and bandaged by him at one time or another. I guess Amy and I were the first three foot tall scarecrows needing to have corn plucked from our noses and ears.

To complete the yearly trifecta, Amy and I once again chose poison over politeness. Our Dad's mother was visiting. Grandmother was a prim and proper widow with medication for her wild heart. After welcoming hugs in the parlor, the big people retired to the dining room for coffee and talk. Before long, her wide-opened purse was underneath the loveseat in the parlor between Amy and me.

Did we close her purse and return the tidy clutch? No, we picked the wrong thing to do, in a unanimous way. We emptied it and opened everything that was closed and ate all the candy. This time we made it all the way to the hospital for a good old fashioned stomach pumping.

Dad was on staff at a hospital in Jackson and would drive in to see his patients when called in for surgery or a birth. One trip he made was of special interest to another physician parking who asked him if he was bringing any of the kids along with him. Dad said he was called in and had work to do, why did he ask? "Well, it looks like there's a little kid on your bumper," said the doctor.

Apparently, even dolls could have a close call on our farm. Brad and Patrice were whooping it up as cowboys and Indians and had tied her tall Raggedy Ann doll to the bumper of Dad's new 1963 Corvair convertible. They quit playing and Brad forgot their captive. The doll had a wild ride to the hospital. Dad's doctor friend never forgot it and always checked Dad's rear bumper with a grin.

A game of hide and seek pushed one doll beyond a close call into the flames of eternity. One variation of the game we played was to hide something of the other's and then watch them look for it, giving hot or cold clues only after the requisite amount of begging and pleading. It was now my turn after a long and merciless morning search for my popgun.

I wanted this to be my best hide yet. Most seven-year-olds might agree that the all time best place to stash something from your siblings is in the wastebasket in the kitchen. Since I took the wastebaskets out as part of my daily "feed the dogs and burn the papers" duties, it was a fine cover for me. I would let my sister's agony run its course and then suddenly "find" the toy they had given up looking for.

As Amy counted to fifty, I hid her current favorite doll, a rag sock monkey with button eyes and long tail. We both had been given one by an aunt. I had my own safely hidden away and stuffed hers deep into the wastebasket. My dear Amy, unable to read her twins mind as easily as those unfortunate identical twins, looked and looked while I remained silent and mocking.

The hiding place lost its ranking that day after someone else took out the papers and burned everything, including Amy's new BFF.

I felt bad about the collateral damage and decided never to hide anything in wastebaskets again. Of course, being alone with my thoughts, it was a hard decision to make.

Junk Pile Treasures

Alex in prize winning 4H float. The capsule was retired to a junk pile behind a barn in 1965 and was visible from earth for over thirty-five years.

photo by Willah Weddon, Women's News Bureau

Explorations around our farm were always about finding interesting places or animals. Junk piles were tops on this list. As preteens we felt we could scavenge any material needed for camping or building forts from the rusty piles of broken or worn out farm hardware. Junk pile stuff was there for the picking, a hardware store/lumber yard at our feet.

My sisters and I hiked far from our farmhouse early one warm January day to investigate a new deposit. Patrice had come across it while horseback riding earlier in October and wanted us to investigate the treasure trove in an old washed out gully in a hayfield with scrub bushes and fast-growing trees around the edge. Twenty feet across and maybe six feet at its deepest, it held a number of rusty barrels, fence wire and what we deduced as contents of a farm shop that lay waiting for a look see.

We had come prepared. I had a short stiff boxsaw, a claw hammer and was wearing my new toy, a green plastic army helmet complete with chin strap and a string netting cover to hold leaves for camouflage. I had been declaring the invincible and protective characteristics of my new headgear during most of the hike.

Amy had a sixteen ounce bottle of pop and a partially full sleeve of saltine crackers for a snack. Patrice carried a twenty foot length of half-inch nylon rope and a pocketknife in her bluejeans. We marched quietly up and through a wooded area bordering our target field and paused before leaving the shade.

Since we had patrolled off our property onto a neighbor's farm, standard procedure called for us to look around and listen a minute or two before stepping into broad daylight. We knew we were welcome to wander but always tried not to leave any obvious tracks or be seen by an adult working the fields. Being invisible was a much sought after skill as a kid.

When spotted by grown ups on machinery, a friendly wave was often followed by an attempt to engage us in a neighborly conversation. "Why, you have grown more than these weeds!" "What are you up to?" "Say hello to your mom and dad," were common refrains issued from the cab of a wheat combine or tractor seat. Sometimes we'd be sent off with a serious "Look out for that bear I saw a few minutes ago!" and a wink.

"Hey, look at that!" Amy whispered as she looked over the open space. A segment of stove pipe radiated skyward from the gully. The kinked end looked like the neck and head of a brontosaurus peering at us as we approached from the wooded trail.

"You go first to see if it chases you," I implored.

"If it does, I'll run right past you in your hunting boots," Amy promised.

We poked, tipped and looked around the irresistible collection. After a few minutes we took a break and were sharing a grape soda.

"Wanna slug?" we would offer, extending the pop bottle to share.

Standing on the rim, surveying the intriguing waste, Amy suggested that it would be cool to cut down the tree next to her using my saw. "And with your so-called battle helmet on, you can have the tree fall on you to see just how good it works," she offered.

There was little to do except back up my claims. "Sounds fine to me," I responded. Amy decided to call me on my boasts and was quickly supported by our older sister, Patrice.

That was how arguments went with them. I never had a chance. It is one reason I enjoy the solitude of nature so much. Double-teaming sisters can do that to a kid.

Patrice tied her rope as far up the tree as she could reach. I started sawing on the three-inch thick trunk and cut out a small wedge. Amy worked away from the other side with the saw. I sat down about ten feet away and drew the rope taut. The tree tipped, and Patrice yodeled, "Timmmmber." I suddenly saw stars and an electric shock ran down my arms and spine. The little tree had landed directly on my plastic helmet and knocked me flat, branches scraping my face.

A moment passed before I dared move, the sobering impact a frightful shock to me. In spite of my proud assessments the plastic helmet afforded no protection. I was more concerned with trying not to cry than anything.

"You must have been really pulling on that tree because it fell faster than any I ever saw," Patrice laughed through the tangle of branches.

Back on our farm, we had a junk pile that was a pretty good spot for jumping cottontail rabbits. The twisted pile of barn wood and roofing metal offered lots of protection from weather and predators. We could always count on at least a hot bunny track to keep the dogs interested.

The top of the pile was the best spot when hunting. From this vantage point we could urge on our dogs that were crawling around and whining earnestly under us. The heap was riddled with rabbit sized runways. Pimpled shot patterns on sheet metal or barn pole testified in support of tales of success and failure.

All the farms around us had piles of junk, usually near property lines. Springtime hikes included a stop over at these sites. A winter's worth of stuff could appear after a season of dormancy and we studied it with an eye to fashioning a sharp-edged weapon or as building materials. As a rule, farmers were frugal and resourceful, so for something to be discarded, it had to have run its course of utility, but was kept around just in case a future use developed. No sense in paying to take it to the township dump.

One neighboring farm had a historic barrel on display behind barns along the paved roadway that split farm from farmhouse. The fifty-five gallon drum had been painted to look like a space capsule and used in a 4H fair parade when I was eleven years old. I was lucky, and small enough, to fit inside it, so was drafted by my club to be the astronaut.

Afterwards, we dismantled our prize-winning float and stacked parts in a pile. For over thirty-five years the rocket ship/barrel remained visible as we drove past. Junk piles don't fade away quickly.

Another growing collection of future valuables lay next to our hilltop farmhouse. One corner of our hill was overgrown and too steep for a tractor to mow or work. At a low spot away from the house, two six-foot steel tractor rear wheels were stacked and used as a burn barrel. This untamed area was affection-ately called over the bank.

It was a handy toss from the back porch to over the bank. Corn cobs, watermelon rinds and chicken bones cartwheeled there during backyard barbeques. Over the bank came to mean the fate of all that was deemed broken, useless, or dead. Missing your cat? Sorry, a car hit her and now she's over the bank.

During the first thaw of spring, a visual, strewn history of our household was revealed on the sloping hillside. I spent many early spring hours plinking away with my BB gun at bottles and cans until the weeds and bushes bloomed enough to obscure the blight. This was the one area on the farm where we never went barefoot.

The thicket was hostile in the summer. Overgrown with poison ivy, nettles, stick-tights, burdocks and sharp needled buckthorn, none of us and few of our dogs would venture over the bank.

Junk piles reflected the growth and decay of farms, and junk piles of my youth aged into lodes of scrap metal. Today, with the price of scrap metal so high, many of the collections have been picked over, easily out-pacing most junk bonds as investments. So maybe "Over the bank" should be changed to "Into the bank."

Barntrained

Riding a runaway horse is a dangerous situation. Both my sisters had to deal with runaway horses and ponies during their riding years on our farm in the 1960s and 70s.

Patrice and my twin sister Amy both rode Western and English styles and often rode bareback. The two knew how to handle horses and this talent at training an animal with the social skills of a four-year-old came in handy when dating and beyond. Show me a girl who can ride, and I'll show you a girl who doesn't have a lot of boy problems.

The two created a steeple chase course through the woods that included jumps over logs of wind blown trees and stacked limbs. The horses got a good workout over trails and hills during the hours my sisters explored the unfenced areas between neighboring farms. They always rode at a walk when getting close to home. The horses knew that relief from their burden, food and water waited. Unless controlled, the horses would increase their speed until they went into a mental zone and bolted. It could be a wild ride back to the farmhouse. A horse that has this nasty habit is referred to as "Barn Trained."

When this happened, riders had to distract or redirect the fleeting beast into an ever shrinking circle. A panicked horse can lose its balance and stumble, or the rider could fall or be knocked off by a tree branch. Not a lot of blood-free options when perched on a half ton of uncontrolled horseflesh running at full speed.

I watched from the front porch one afternoon as my twin on a flighty gelding galloped home along the roadway. I heard them first, a cloppity, clappity, clippity of hoof on pavement and the grunting hunt, hunt of a horse laboring for speed.

They came angling into our gravel driveway, overshot it and started up the hill toward the porch. She let him have it there, and jerked his head to one side with the reins. He skidded and kicked up some of the dried lawn. Amy kept his head tucked and under control as they twirled around, stopping by the tack area in the garage across the driveway. After clipping lines to both sides of his bridle bit, she walked away and stood a moment to catch her breath. We never rode him home along the road again.

Patrice was thrown from her runaway Arabian mix one early spring day. She was up on her easy riding bay mare, Amadore's Star, and turned for home after a nice ride through field and swale. Amadore was lathered up from the workout and Patrice was gently reining her along a tractor path through marsh grass and up into an open field. Beneath the tallest tree on the property, a poplar with a trunk so big, my sisters and I could hold hands and not reach around it, the two turned homeward.

As Amadore leveled off on more solid ground, the mare decided it was time to run for the barn. Her speed went from a picking walk to a cantor and when on open ground shifted into an outright gallop. Patrice felt the horse's muscle's gather and tense, and knowing her mare was escalating into a bolt, took the slack out of her reins and pulled, trying to regain control, or at least get Amadore's attention. No response,

Within a few paces the horse was racing toward an opening in a tree line between fields where stretched an unseen single strand of barbed wire. Patrice pulled on a rein with all her might, bringing the horse's nose back to her stirrup. But the horse charged on.

The wire caught Amadore inches above her front legs, stretched and then stiffened, pulling the horse down and throwing Patrice forward into the winter wheat stubble.

When Patrice came to, Amadore was standing and bleeding. Three strips of flesh hung from a football-sized gash across the front of her chest.

The veterinarian sewed the layers of muscles together and closed the wound. Most of the family was gathered in the field around the standing horse. "We'll see, but I don't think she will ever be all good to run or jump," Doc Spencer said solemnly as he wiped his hands and put away his instruments, closing his leather medical bag with a snap. "Going full out like that, she could have cut herself much deeper, but she's a tough ol' girl," he added.

"That's why they use horse hide for making baseballs," I contributed. Dad allowed that it would be a while before we played catch with Amadore's hide.

Patrice was sore for a few days, but other than that, survived that close call with no physical after effects. Amadore responded well to my sister's constant care and by the next summer, had recovered from her trauma enough to ride and jump.

SUMMER

Summer Underground

Digging tunnels became a most enjoyable pastime in the 1960s when hot summer days replaced the cooler Michigan springtime. With the sun hanging higher and the days longer, flowing waters slowed and lowered, making it easier for our wandering gang of almost-teens to jump over creeks and drainage ditches.

Most creek banks were overgrown with brush and thistle with the occasional open spaces of marsh grass. These open spaces were preferred by muskrats and my friends for digging tunnels. Late one July, Richie, Larry and I were making our way to a spot Larry claimed to have potential. When we came upon it, Richie didn't waste any time and fell to his knees in the black muck, pulling out fistful after fistful of fibrous swamp grass and clearing a work area in the creek bank. About half way up the eight foot embankment, black muck met sandy soil in a horizontal line.

Larry had his dad's World War II trenching tool. He unfolded it into a nifty little shovel and handed it to Richie. The boy could dig like a badger. He'd spear into the soft dirt with the tool, breaking loose soil and cutting roots or picking stones. After a few pokes, moving deeper in, he would scoop the waste, haul it back and dump it behind him so Larry and I could get at it.

It was quick work and soon the determined Richie was in so deep only his ankles and feet were visible - the danger zone in our subterranean ingressions. Eventually, all our tunnels caved in. We made sure the digger kept at least one foot or ankle exposed, giving us something to grip and pull him from under cascading earth.

Across the ditch, their dog Queenie hit a hot track and ran baying into the twenty acre untilled field between our homes. We took a break and followed her for a while, then hauled up at the latest shelter made by the two's talented and woods-wise older brother. Denny had made a hut using ragweeds that grew tall and straight in the old field. He cut and tied the long weeds into uniform bundles that reminded me of marble columns. The ragweed shelter was as beautiful as the Greek Parthenon to me.

Richie and Larry declared that they were going back to the new tunnel. I hiked home to get a small garden spade from our garage/corncrib and headed back to the excavation ready for some close-in work with the tool.

Queenie met me in the field and we tromped together along the path through weeds that towered over us. Blackbirds were warbling and a slight breeze moved the swamp grass in waves. I jumped across and made my way to the site. It was pretty quiet at the new dig. Queenie was already sniffing around and trotted on as I came into the clearing.

The entire bank had caved in, spilling dirt into the cleared area. I wasn't sure what to think. Were Larry and Richie under everything? I didn't see any tracks or signs of a resurrection. To be sure, I clawed away sandy loam and muck, in search of body parts. I tired, stopped and decided I should have found them by now.

I climbed up the bank and went towards their house, a hundred yards away. I studied the lawn as I approached. Nobody out there. I couldn't hear anything when I made the yard and was starting to wonder what I was going to say. I kicked the aluminum storm door a few times and soon heard Larry say, "Come on in."

I told him about the tunnel caving in.

"Really? Man, it's good thing you weren't in it when it happened, huh?" observed Larry.

"I got the shovel," I answered, and decided not to tell him of my heroic rescue efforts.

Between Larry, me and our siblings some kind of creative above ground on the ground or under the ground construction project was always underway in our neighborhood. Future archeologists, studying our ruins, will probably declare the area a major population center of small, warlike humanoids.

We had tree houses, ground-based blinds, forts, lean-to's, straw and hay huts, shelters and underground tunnels. No matter what it was made of or what the elevation, the assemblage of scrap and natural materials was always referred to as a "hut."

We even had a platform braced across the inside of a large culvert that channeled a shallow creek under a road. The cement tube was cave-like and big. I had to stand and reach up to touch the ceiling.

This creek hut was the ideal gathering place during the summer because it was always cool. The waters and shade along with occasional breezes kept temperatures low. We used candle smoke to write names and other creative notes on the poured concrete of the culvert's ceiling.

After hours of the summer sun, it was a welcome retreat. Larry and I would recline on the old barn boards with our backs against the arching sides and feel our body heat wick away into the concrete. Cars and trucks rumbled ten feet overhead as they slowed for the nearby intersection. We'd sit and watch dragonflies flit by. Barn swallows sliced through the center of the tube. We could easily see Sickle back minnows, frogs, crayfish and bottom crawling insects through the clear running water. Now and then turtles would paddle by. The display of nature was always interesting and never boring. Better than any movie, we'd claim to each other.

The acoustics of the place made it easy to hear each other above the riffling water. We talked in hushed tones over the chirping concert of crickets and buzzing locusts.

Amy and neighbor Ann joined us and put two cans of pop into the water to cool. The can tops looked different.

"Look at this, it's pretty neat, you don't need a can opener, just pull up on this tab and there ya go," explained Ann. She opened her can, click, pop, fishhh it went. The triangular opening went from rim to the top's center.

"Check this out," she continued, and put the aluminum ring tab on her finger, extending her arm to show it off.

"That's perfect for camping, next time we go, we gotta get some pop like that," declared Larry and the conversation jumped to planning our next underground campout.

Saved by a Torpedo

The horse fort in August. A desolate apple tree and Scottish thistles accent the barren, old barn siding look. Sharing the hut with horses made Alex nervous.

    The most serious of all my underground mis-adventures happened when I was digging an escape tunnel. I was alone and trapped at the age of eleven.

    My sisters Patrice and Amy and I had built an enclosure of four walls and a rag roof near our new pole barn using materials from the demolished old barn. Using post hole diggers, we stabbed away at the sun-baked hard pan of the pasture until we had holes deep enough for the long poles that once supported the roof. The wood had served over seventy years as rafters of the old barn and were in good shape. Worms had eaten designs into the surfaces that looked like mysterious runes, and we creatively translated the squiggles into messages from the ancient ones, complete with hand gestures and sing-song notes.

The four walls of our latest hut were fashioned from old barn wood tacked or tied to the corner posts. Amy gathered old burlap grain sacks for the roof and we tied them together with baler twine to make a fine sun shade. They furled in the gusts and breezes, slapping and making noises like a sail.

It was our most recent refuge to gather and tell stories and sometimes use as a WWII HQ in combat. When dirt clods were seen in the firing lanes, the barrels of our BB guns poked from the punched out knot holes to save the day and change the tide of the war.

The enclosure was strong enough to thwart attacks from monster kid-eating shrews, but lucky to withstand a summer gusher and blow.

It was called the horse fort because it had no door, and our horses could amble in anytime. The curious beasts walked in at will to investigate our secret meetings. After a breeze caused the burlap roof to flap and snap the animals spun and bolted out. Ducking away from the skewing hooves, I could see the advantage of an escape route.

I had a healthy respect for horses thanks to the creative efforts of my two sisters. They loved to ride and torment me from the backs of the animals. The girls rode around the pastures and fields of the farm, and wouldn't hesitate to act at the behest of a parent to find me, often in the woods with my BB gun and hound. It only took two of them on horses to surround me.

The girls could handle horses, and I think those years of experience helped them greatly in their dealings with men. According to Patrice, horses and adolescent boys share the same level of maturity and respond well to directions supported by a boot to the ribs.

The fort needed an escape tunnel, for sure. I picked the corner farthest from the door and drew a small circle, just my size. With the clay being so hard, I wasn't about to make extra work enlarging a hole that only I would use.

The digging was difficult. The packed clay yielding begrudgingly to any tool my eighty pound body would put against it. I had seen packed soil like this before when I started scratching out a cave in the basement of our 1880's farmhouse.

That project began in the area of the basement we retreated to in times of impending tornadoes. The yellow soil was dry and hard as stone. After trying a butter knife, pitch fork, and garden shovel to no avail, I tried my brother's Boy Scout hatchet, and it worked great. I began chopping and chipping a cave of good size, generously allowing room for the whole family. My attempt to insert a progress report of this caring act of foresight into a dinner conversation resulted in Dad inspecting my work.

"We can't have you burrowing into the foundation and causing our home to collapse, " he pointed out with a hint of exasperation, "So dig somewhere else."

With the horse fort project, my logistics dictated I start two holes. The dig was on for them to meet below the wall. After hours of work over a few days, I poked through. The two shafts were off by a few inches but had to do, I was sick of chipping away and digging.

The new hole was little more than a slot large enough for my head and an arm. I put one arm ahead of me and the other along my side and wormed myself into the narrow cave.

Feeling a rush of success, I dug my toes into the clay and pushed ahead, expecting to scrape through and up. My toes slipped from the effort and I paused to plan my next move. I wasn't going any farther ahead. It was a tight fit and I couldn't move. I was wedged in. I had to breathe in short, shallow breaths. Too tight for sure, this will need more work, I assessed and put it in reverse but I couldn't go backwards either. Here I was with one arm pressed along the side of my sweating face and the other trapped along my side. I had to wriggle my arm to let light in.

What do I do next? I wondered. The hatchet was on the surface, near my exposed feet. I was in past my knees and couldn't reach beyond them.

Sammy, a friendly quarter horse, sauntered up to my exposed canvas tennis shoes. "It won't be long now and the other horses will come over and get excited," I guessed. They always acted jumpy when something new was in their world and my giant red "worms" waving from a hole in the ground would set them off, for sure. Their stomping around would cave in the tunnel, I predicted behind eyes pinched shut against fear, sand and sweat.

The one tool that might help me dig, a little black plastic torpedo, was jammed in my back pocket. It was the only one left of those that shot from the bathtime submarine toy my brothers had handed down to me. The little arrow would shoot underwater from spring loaded torpedo tubes. I had taken the liberty to sharpen its point with a nail file for use in this project. I started working my hand back to the rear pocket and let my breath out as much as I could to make room for my arm. I grasped the four inch plastic shaft and started jabbing. My fingers weakened and I dropped the torpedo a few times. But I was able to chip away and move just a bit, my confidence growing and my fear receding with each jab. After half an hour, I had to rest a moment.

Sammy put his head down and blew into the tunnel. He had a habit of nipping anything red and lifting it up. Convinced he was deciding which red PF Flyer to grab, I kicked and wriggled with renewed urgency and dislodged myself enough to inch back. My shirt gathered up, exposing my back as I wriggled out. Sammy, his head lowered to my level, peered at me in the bright daylight.

That week, Amy declared the hole a danger to her horses and wanted it filled. I was outside the fort, helping her toss rocks and dirt into the tunnel and told her of my close call when making the escape hatch.

"Why don't you just push this bottom board away and crawl out like I do?" She answered from inside, her boot easily pushing the unfastened board away from the corner post over my filled tunnel.

Dog Days of Summer

In the 1960s, if a store had air conditioning, it advertised the fact to draw in customers. It was a big attraction. The 1890s farmhouse I grew up in, like most homes at the time, did not have air conditioning, unless you count standing in front of the refrigerator with the door wide open. It did have nine foot ceilings and was shaded by a number of hardwood trees. When a humid summer heat wave settled in, the second story temperatures melted the enforced civility between my brothers and sisters.

With five kids in three upstairs bedrooms trying to sleep in the heat, many options were investigated. Two that didn't make it were having a younger sibling stand by your bed, waving a cardboard fan, the other, buying an in-ground pool. Somewhere between the costs of those two, Dad decided to put an exhaust fan in the window at the head of the stairs. It would suck out the stale upstairs air while drawing in air from the open windows of the bedrooms. The fan's motor would labor and then rattle and hum. The old window sill would chatter then subside, then chatter again in a drawn out rhythm. The mechanical noise drowned out all outside sounds and seemed relentless to me. I dreamt of things mechanical instead of the usual dreams of open fields and flying.

My single bedroom was nearest the fan window, down the hallway along the staircase from my brother's bedroom. When the fan was laboring and sleep was slipping over my consciousness, a brother would declare he was sending one my way and soon an ungrateful odor would billow by, causing me to press my ten-year-old cheeks against my bedroom's only window screen and complain about the air quality.

During the hottest time of the year, physical activity was reduced to a minimum. Just going to the bathroom could cause a person to break a sweat. At night, we all slept on our backs to keep forehead sweat from running into our eyes. Instead, rivulets of sweat gathered along creases between skin and pillow. Lack of sleep and the heat made my brothers and sisters grumpy.

Our free range farm dogs would scratch a cool spot in the shade, then plop down and pant. They would look about with a hint of aloofness, accented by the occasional snap at a strafing horsefly. When the evening temperature dropped into the 70s, cicadas would call in their rattlesnake-like sound and continue into the early morning hours. The night bugs each had their own sounds and frequencies. Patient listening revealed many different insect calls.

With no air conditioning in the family station wagon, road trips to see the grandparents could be a real test for Mom and Dad. Not long after leaving the driveway and up to cruising speed, we would adjust the windows for the maximum air flow. Soon after, one of us would pipe up over the roaring wind and ask how much longer before we got there. "We'll be there soon, dear," Mom would reassure. We all knew the 100 mile trip would be well over two hours and wondered if the heat had affected her sense of time.

Soon thirst and what a drink of ice cold pop would taste like were the topics of conversation in the back seats. Sensing a moment to torment, an older brother would repeat a sing song taunting of "cool water, cool, cool water."

The effect on my young mind was powerful. I could only think of pools of bubbling clear spring water and desperately wanted to quench my now overwhelming thirst. Begging them to stop would often result in one's being the other's slave for a negotiated amount of days.

After days of sweltering heat, we were driven to the point of pleading with others to do our chores. These plaintive bleatings were often issued while reclining on our vinyl covered sofa in the path of moving humid air from an antique floor fan. This was the most sought after place in the farmhouse on those evenings when the heat just hung in the air. Calling it safe when you left for a moment meant nothing, it was a matter of seniority and comfort to my older sister and brothers.

We all had chores. One of mine was to feed and water the hunting dogs kept in a pen across the lawn from the back door. With the air so full of moisture, a temperature drop into the mid-70s would cause a dewfall. This usually happened after sunset, and coincided with my canine duties.

A single mercury lamp high over the pasture gate cast its blue-green colored light over the barnyard and house. The bright light cast my stark shadow that jumped and stretched as I moved across the uneven lawn. I carried the bucket of dog food with my left hand, keeping my right hand free to open the dogs pen and ready to fend off imagined attackers waiting in the clammy shadows at the yards edge.

One August night, I had closed and latched the dog pen gate and was meandering slowly back to the farmhouse. I was wearing bellbottom jeans and trying not to get them wet from the fresh dew on the grass. I must have almost stepped on a frog because the cold blooded beast leapt full force up my left leg bellbottom to behind my knee and kept thrusting upward with its back legs. The sensation brought on a sudden and intense sense of clarity.

I had seen a Western movie where a cowboy wakes up from his night's sleep by the campfire and has a Diamondback rattlesnake alongside him under his horse blanket. My racing mind easily made the connection and determined that a Massasauga rattler had bushwhacked me.

I kicked stiff legged in abject terror. By now, I was convinced the rattler was trapped in my pant leg and urgently injecting every last drop of venom into my leg. I karate kicked, then I hopped on one leg while spastically jerking the sacrificial leg. No success.

Between whirling and kicking, I looked back at the dog pen. The two Brittanys hadn't even stopped eating and here I was fighting for my life. I planned to repay their loyalty in their next feeding, if I lived that long.

I kicked an imaginary football and felt the reptile slide from my pantleg and launch into the night. The mercury light revealed a cartwheeling blue-green leopard frog, and not the three foot long pit viper I expected. A giddy elation replaced panic. I ran to the porch and sat, breathless and sweat soaked from my latest close call.

A Lucky Toss

Against all odds, the gas tank did not blow up in flames when a snug firecracker exploded. Alex at fifteen on his Honda 90.

photo by E.R. Weddon, MD, Spring, 1970.

To me, as a sixteen-year-old in the early 1970s, the end of the school year meant freedom from keeping track of time or day. The 4th of July was an exception. That date was always a celebration of our firecracker and bottle rocket skills. Years of experience with these dangers gave my friends and brothers confidence and bravado. A combination that opens the door to accidents.

My older brothers would lay in a supply of firecrackers and bottle rockets when they would drive to Ohio to buy 3.2 beer or take sheep to market. Todd and Brad bought explosives. The sizzling, whistling or smoking fireworks just didn't have the appeal of a powerful blast. After taking lambs to market in their '55 Chevy stake bed truck, they would return late at night with a few dollars, tales of adventure with Ohio girls and glory be, brown paper sacks full of firecrackers.

Rare and expensive big boomers like Silver Salutes or M-80's were held in awe. The M-80 had a heft to it. Even it's name sounded military and war-like. It was made with a hard, red cardboard tubing sealed with green wax and a one inch fuse sticking from the middle that would burn underwater. The Silver Salute was about the same size, but the tubing was colored silver. An attractive look, but not all business like the M-80's red.

The explosives were subject to confiscation on sight or rumor by our mother. She already had her hands full dealing with our flesh wounds, bites, burns and broken bones. Trying to repair a finger or two that had been shredded by 80 grains of dynamite was something she was going to avoid at all costs. Mom was frugal, though, she wouldn't throw away the contraband, but kept it hidden away safely, along with the squirt guns and switchblades extracted from the clenched fists of her little angels.

Black Cat firecrackers in packs of 20 or strings of 100 were carefully unraveled into single hand deployed units. The goal was to have the explosion in mid air, allowing for the maximum sound and carry, not to mention surprise. At times, a situation would require that two or three fuses be braided together and lit as one. The extra firepower was needed to overcome the loss of surprise, like when around a campfire or in a rowboat. The fuse powder would color our fingers silver, not too unlike the glitter many school kids sprinkle on themselves today to look cool.

Knowing when to toss a single was gained from experience. The 'crackers exploded in the middle, so we made it a practice of gently holding the end of the firecracker between thumb and first finger. Using a Zippo lighter borrowed from our parents was not the choice for lighting solo shots. The wide flame easily started the fuse in its middle, necessitating a hasty and inaccurate toss. A lighter was fine when touching off a whole pack, as the first explosion sometimes blew out the central fuse. Igniting many fuses ensured complete combustion.

One particular 4th of July I was riding my motorcycle following my friends Larry and Ricky. They were in Larry's 1964 Mercury Comet and we were going into town for the big celebration and fireworks at the school football field.

Trying to light a firecracker in a moving car took some preparation. Using knowledge gained from ear ringing bad judgement and painful lack of foresight, a procedure evolved that incorporated safety and ignorance.

First, all the rear windows had to go up, and the exit window, the one next to the 'cracker man, was cranked down. Using a car's cigarette lighter was the ignition system of choice. Once the lighter was pushed on, the fuses of one or two firecrackers would be straightened and one would be held ready to touch the red hot lighter. When the fuse smoked, the ordnance was flung out the opening in a sweeping move, letting go as the arm extended out the window. Then back for the second. If quick enough, you could touch off a pair in rapid succession before the lighter went cold. Follow through was important, as firecrackers were known to find a way back into the car.

We had been fine-tuning our technique of flame and fling and felt pretty confident our skills would be appreciated by the townspeople and law officers.

Larry and Ricky decided to lead the way to town in the car while I followed on my motorcycle. Dust swirled and gravel flew as they boiled out of Larry's driveway. From my motorcycle I could see Ricky light a Black Cat firecracker and flick it out the window of the accelerating Comet. Bang! I laughed out loud in my helmet and zigged and zagged a little to show my approval. Ricky's arm was out the window and tossed another. I didn't see the smoke trail of the fuse, but waited.

The firecracker landed on my motorcycle's seat, right between my crotch and gas tank and exploded, catching me completely off guard. My hands left the handlebars in reflex and I looked down in fright. The bike nosedived a bit with the loss of throttle and I pitched forward. Everything looked intact, but I deferred greater inspection until after regaining control of the bike and composure.

The red Comet sped away and was showing signs of pilot error. Larry and Rick were falling into each other laughing and slapping high-fives. They pulled over and I caught up to them, holding back until I could see they weren't lighting anything else.

"We didn't see where it went, but were looking at you when it went off, and couldn't believe our luck!" gasped a leaky-eyed Ricky.

As the years went by, firecrackers became weaker and harder to find. My brothers had laid up a decent stash of them, but by the mid-1970s, the supply had been exhausted. There was a resurgence when I found the hidden lode Mom had ferreted away. But all too soon, the black Cats, Zebras, M-80s and rare Silver Salutes were gone. It's probably just as well. Otherwise, this close call on the farm may have been typed quite a bit slower.

Attacked by a Donkey

Sister Patrice on Pokey, a donkey that reacted violently to a newborn foal.

A donkey tried to kill my Dad. The attack happened in the barnyard of our farm, one early afternoon many years ago. Dad had returned from his medical office for lunch. He also wanted to check on the progress of repairing the barnyard fence started by my brothers Todd and Brad three months earlier.

His Quarter horse mare, Daydream, was due to foal any day, and he wanted work around the barn finished. She was a thick barreled, gentle trail horse and carried a western brand. Dad often rode the sorrel-colored mare, watching the farm's wildlife unfold just over her perked up ears.

Today he was on his way down the flagstone walk from the house when he heard the panicked squeals of Daydream. His horse was trotting and whinnying in bursts of hysterical despair. He couldn't locate her but saw the farm donkey, Pokey, in the barnyard down on its front knees with a glistening newborn under its jacking chin. The donkey was working her knees onto the baby and biting it in a blind frenzy.

Dad vaulted the gate and closed on the grunting donkey, now looking at him and rising. Dad went one way and the donkey moved with him, keeping the newborn near its back feet.

Looking over the donkey into the pasture beyond this standoff, Dad saw Daydream bolting in a circle. She slowed when approaching the fence. The new mother stopped, dropped her head and flopped to the ground.

Before Dad could check out what was troubling the mare, the donkey lunged at him. He smacked the animal just under its eye and dodged out of the way, taking a position closer to the baby. The donkey spun and drove at him again. This time Dad came around with a fist and drove it between the eight hundred pound animal's nostrils. The donkey took a step back, shook its head and snorted. Dad took advantage of the moment to push the quaking foal under the fence, out of reach of the donkey. As he finished, Pokey was on him again, clenching her teeth into Dad's back, just over his left shoulder blade. She lifted my father onto his feet and jerked him to one side. The fingers of Dad's left hand clutched a top fence board, and he steadied himself. Leveraging his weight, he reached down to grab a scrap length of a four-by-four post. The donkey yanked Dad off his feet but he twisted and broke free of her bite. Falling backwards, he planted his feet and swung hard at Pokey's jaw.

My father packed a mean swing. When in high school, he was varsity baseball team batting champion three years in a row. He was invited, with other high school standouts to take batting practice in Tiger Stadium and once told me how he'd hit balls into the centerfield stands. The sawed off four by four wasn't exactly a bat, but the oncoming light-colored snout bristling with teeth wasn't a fastball either. He swung for the fences and drove that donkey back on her haunches. Her head lolled to one side.

82

The homerun blast seemed to settle things between Dad and Pokey for a moment. He side- stepped through the fenceboards, kicked the barnyard gate closed, and cradled the newborn. Eyeing the now docile donkey in the barnyard, he made his way to Daydream. There he knelt down with the baby and choked out a cry. Daydream lay dead in the noonday sun. It had been an emotional three or four minutes, too much for the traumatized mare's heart.

Dad secured the little one, a colt, in a dry and safe stall, then trudged to to the farmhouse to call the vet and change his shredded clothes. In this warmer weather, he wore sleeveless t-shirts under a short-sleeved white dress shirt. He returned to his office and waiting patients. The first patient to see my father went pale.

"Doc," he gasped. "You're back's covered in blood." The back of Dad's fresh shirt bore a darkening blot of maroon.

The donkey had taken a chunk out of his back the size of a deck of cards, and yet he still didn't feel it. Maybe the adrenaline hadn't worn off. More likely, he was overwhelmed with emotion. Dad cancelled his afternoon appointments and drove himself to Foote

Hospital in Jackson, twenty miles away, to be sewn up.

He returned home that afternoon, a little sore, but with chores to do. Dad put a log chain around Daydream's neck and pulled her with our tractor to the north end of the farm. He buried her near where the two of them often pulled up to watch the sun set across open fields and wood. Daydream standing peacefully looking westward, a rear fetlock cocked and resting. Dad in his saddle, reins draped across the pommel, savoring a pipeful of tobacco.

At the vet's recommendation, we confined Pokey and watched her for signs of rabies. After a few days confinement, she was pronounced clear and arrangements were made to get rid of her. Dad said the animal went back to the farm where she came from. I thought otherwise. For years afterward, the image of that beast's hooves came to mind whenever I used brown glue.

We named the colt Little Red Sambo, or Sammy, for short, and bottle-fed him with fresh milk from neighboring farms. He grew to be part of the family. Amy and Patrice doted on him. They filled quart bottles (we used old green Squirt pop bottles) with a milk blend and put large black nipples on them to feed the hungry colt.

Sammy made every effort to follow us around the farm and yard. He even spent some time in our house, against Mom's protests. For some reason, my sisters used that experience to start a tradition of walking all new horses through the back door into the dining room and living room, then out parlor's front door. Mom appeared particularly concerned when the stony hooves danced over the parlor's oriental rug. After what kittens, puppies, cats and dogs had done to it, she didn't care to deal with a super-sized pile of road apples.

Sammy proved to be an energetic and curious little guy. The gangly red-haired colt could not resist following my father as he worked around the barn or pasture. Watching over Dad's shoulder, the orphan waited until the man seemed to pay no attention to him. Then Sammy nipped ever so cautiously around Dad's back pocket to tug out a red bandanna, lift it high and wave it, nickering playfully. The little rascal made it a habit, and soon Dad decided to play along, tucking bandannas in both back pockets. Sammy grew to be larger and stockier than any of the other foals we'd raised on the farm. He proved to be easy to break and trail ride, and he brought home championship ribbons from horse shows. He never much cared for donkeys, though.

Sometimes, when all of us went swimming in the farm lake, we noticed the deep scar on Dad's back. We marveled at how he fought a near-ton, raging donkey to save Sammy. A hero, for sure.

"I'll bet if he could have reached the gaping hole in his back he would have stitched himself up," Brad wagered. We nodded to each other in agreement.

The Long Days of Summer Vacation

Every spring as the days grew longer, chatting school mates counted down the last days of the school year with greater frequency. Soon the long days of classes will be replaced with the short days of summer break.

Kids wondering why their summer vacation goes by so quickly should be asked what time of day they get out of bed.

To make the days seem longer, try getting up at dawn and keep up a steady pace until sunset. Out West cowboys call it "working from can 'til can't." A few sun drenched weeks of that and the summer will grow to an eon in your memory.

Winter wheat is harvested in early summer and the wheat straw is baled and put up in a barn. For a number of mornings as a thirteen-year-old lying in bed, I heard the neighboring farmer's old John Deere tractor chugga chugging along the road past our house, pulling one or sometimes two wagons loaded with straw bales enroute to a big barn a quarter mile away. This was my alarm clock and opportunity knocking all at once.

I threw my light blanket to the foot of my bed and over my startled beagle and leapt into my scattered pants, socks and work boots. The tractor was still approaching as I dashed downstairs, out the door and jumped on my bike. If I pedaled like crazy I could catch and meet him at the big barn and help unload the first bale from the wagon. Since it was straw and not hay, the bales were light and easy for a little fella like me to handle, and to top it off, I could earn some cash. Richie and Larry arrived on their bikes from their home across from the barn. The barn owner's daughters, Ann and Jane, came and watched, being too young to help out.

Farmer Doug positioned himself by the controls of the tractor. The motor powered a steel shaft attached to the hay conveyor or elevator. At times it seemed his eyes were looking in different directions from trying to keep track of all the youngsters wandering around the moving and potentially dangerous equipment. He'd make sure all was clear, then rev up the tractor and throw a lever forward to engage the elevator. Doug climbed onto the wagonload and tossed the bales onto the screeching, cleated track of the elevator. The golden bales clickity-clicked up the long metal channel in the bright morning sun, then into the shade of the barn. As the bales tumbled off, we quickly inspected them to for prickers, vetch (we called it "itchy-stuff") or snakes dangling out. Picking up a bale to find a reptile writhing under the twine was sure to cause a jump and cuss.

We stacked the straw onto the well-worn oak floors of the hip-roofed barn, and neatly stacked bales soon covered our make-shift basketball court, BB gun shooting range, trapeze and theater that the empty barn decks had provided us during the winter and early spring months.

Hundreds of bales stacked up and up during the day. Then a wagon left the barn for more bales, and we took a break, rinsing our arms and faces with a water hose. Then, with the water its coldest and most refreshing, we gulped long drinks.

Ann and Jane sometimes brought their battery operated AM radio into the barn. The new Lee Dorsey hit song, "Working in the Coal Mine," prompted us to sing along, though we substituted the phrase, "working in the hay loft."

While waiting, we joked, made dares and told stories of monster sightings. A dozen pigeons came flapping into the barn. The elevator racket and tumbling bales had spooked them out of the rafters and onto the barn roof.

About the time the old barn had settled back to normal, we'd hear the tractor laboring up the small hill to the intersection near the barn.

After a few days of this work and reward, the barn looked stuffed. Doug stood on an empty wagon and kicked a loose clump of straw onto the bare ground. "The field's finished," he declared. He paid us a dollar each and rumbled back to his farm, leaving the golden mountain to us. It was the day we had waited for. We knew snow would cover the fields before we'd hear that tractor coming to retrieve some straw. Until then, the barn was under our dominion. We slaked our thirst with a cool drink before putting our latest secret plan into action.

A weak afternoon breeze pushed between the shrunken barn siding, creating a mix of low, soughing and sometimes whistling sounds. The retiring tractor chug-chugged in the distance between the soothing expirations.

With new-found energy, we went to work re-arranging hundreds of bales. Our blueprint, refined throughout the day, included long zigzag tunnels leading to a secret pit at the top of the loft. For the ceiling of our secret hut, we placed long boards across the hole with bales stacked across them, flush with the top tier of the loft.

The main tunnel ran the length of the hay loft, then made a u-turn and came back. We built pits that dropped six feet, dead-ends and even made a false room to give interlopers the impression they had found our mystery fortress. The tunnel to the genuine straw fort lay behind a false bale end

It was Larry's idea to make it look like a real bale. He took a six inch portion of a broken bale, tied it with twine and plugged it into the real tunnel. To the untrained eye, it was impossible to tell this door from the other, full sized bales stacked next to and around it. This was our most magnificent hay hut of all time.

With access to the secret fort now secure, we jumped on our one-speed bikes and pedaled toward town, about three miles away, for bottles of pop. We rode single-file down the middle of the road, seeing who could roll their tires on the centerline stripe the longest.

Finally returning to the barn with our glass bottles dripping of condensation, along with candy cigarettes and potato chips, the three of us settled into our newest secret lair and enjoyed the fruits of our long day's labor.

One side of our new retreat was the barn wall. The shrunken boards allowed shafts of sunlight in and also much welcomed fresh air. Our junk food diet caused emissions of such volume that we may very well have started global warming. Who knew?

With the strenuous work and six miles of biking, there wasn't a lot of energy for much else but reclining in the straw fortress and swapping lies.

After dark the we split up and straggled home summer-tired. I flopped into bed and snuggled into the cool side of my pillow. My dirty fingers plucked stems of straw from my hair. The reminder brought on a replay of the day's adventure beginning with the cough-cough-cough of a two lunged John Deere announcing the start of another long day of the longest summer.

Happy Ram

My second oldest brother, Brad, raised an award-winning flock of sheep in the mid-1960s. He was most determined to raise sheep for wool and market after helping and witnessing our oldest brother earn money on a regular basis. Todd was successful in raising a few head of Hereford steers and cows and along with running a trapline, had money for cars and parts.

Seeing Todd's financial fountain grow, Brad focused on a plan to make as much money on the farm, with less effort. "No half-ton beast stepping on my boots," he once reflected when asked why he went in the sheep and not the cattle business.

I was almost a teenager when Brad and Todd navigated our farm's rickety old stake bed truck along dusty gravel roads, pavement and segments of highway north of Lansing to Harrison to purchase three Corriedale rams. Brad had already brokered a deal with a fellow 4H Club member for two and had the best pick for himself.

The fearless brothers drove the dilapidated truck far beyond its limits. As dusk fell, transmission problems left them stuck on the side of a country road a few miles short of their destination.

Todd swung himself under the truck for an up-close look. Brad stood on the gravel shoulder, plucked a burdock leaf to shade his eyes and looked up and down the quiet road. The old engine gurgled and ticked as it cooled in the fading light. Todd rolled out from under the transmission, stood up and stretched, looking over the countryside.

"It's the linkage all right. I can fix it with some of that electric fencing in the back," Todd declared confidently. His keen eye zeroed in on a lonely rusty vehicle a quarter mile away in a nearby field.

"That junk truck is the same make and year as ours," he said to Brad who was gathering tools from the cab floor, "and I'm sure the tranny is the same."

In less time than it takes these days to get a mechanic to call back with an estimate, the resourceful lads managed to scavenge enough parts to fix their fragmented transmission with one flashlight and a handful of tools. Then they drove on..

The boys proudly pulled into our barnyard, honking and shouting above the engine's overheated roar. "We bought three fine rams, and I named mine Happy Ram," Brad said. "and he is a beauty." The ram settled right in with the dozen ewes. He became their leader, protector and easily took on the role of harem master. As simple minded as sheep are, Happy Ram had personality and enjoyed the company and well-earned respect of Brad and his friends.

The big sheep did have his eccentricities, though. A more notable one was his immediate and powerful head butting of anything challenging his reign. Knowing this, Brad chided his friends to get down to Happy's eye level to say howdy. Time after hilarious time, the animal drove his hornless head into Brad's slow reacting buddies.

Happy Ram had zero tolerance of other rams. One unfortunate temporary boarder, a younger Corriedale ram, was knocked senseless by the senior ram, walking sideways ever after. Brad paid the owner a fair price for the off-kilter and docile ram and promptly named him Charlie Brown. The ram lived out his days with the herd in a peaceful daze.

Another trait, or affliction depending on one's proximity to the ram, was his profuse production of nasal mucus that caused a string of snot to grow like an icicle from his broad snout. As the sticky stalactite reached critical mass, the wooly fellow reset the process by whipping his head back and forth until a twirling string of goober slime cartwheeled through the air. He rarely lobbed any on his own regal frame.

This talent first came to light shortly after Happy Ram's arrival. Brad was eager to impress his latest girlfriend with his animal husbandry skills and future as a wool magnate. The handsome farm boy led the young lady, delicate and somewhat new to farm life, across the barnyard and into the pasture to his prized purchase.

Seeing his new friend bringing what looked like an addition to his harem, Happy Ram sauntered up to meet them. He heard Brad's introduction with indifference, then huffed and snapped his head to and fro. A long rope of glistening mucus slapped across her dress from waist to knees, prompting an imme-diate and overcoming effect on her diminutive demeanor. Brad had heard his share of locker room talk and our father could unleash a string of epithets that prompted many a dog to tuck tail and flee, but Brad was shocked to hear the coarse verbiage issue from the refined and upright woman of breeding.

Brad and Happy Ram outlasted that diversion and the two proudly won a grand champion ribbon at the county fair. As summer waned, my brother was eager to see how he stacked up against other champion rams from around the state, and he prepared for the final fair of the year, the Michigan State Fair on Woodward Avenue in Detroit.. Brad's plan for world domination was unfolding on schedule. "He'll win, and my name will be broadcast on the PA systems all over the fairgrounds, "Brad crowed. "Yup, I'll be famous and plenty of farmers will call to pay me good money for Happy Ram's attention.".

Brad carefully studied the show arena, picking a slight elevation to help accentuate Happy Ram's conformation when standing him before the judges. The farm boy had picked up a few tips by studying other winners and ring judges in action. Familiarization and preparation were two practiced components of his efforts. Brad spent as much time trimming and blocking his prized animal as he did his own hair. "And with similar amazing results," he countered when teased about his preening. His white show shirt hung over his tack box, wrinkle free until moments before entering the ring. Then the call came over the Public Address for the state championship class. Brad checked his perfectly combed hair, then blotted the afternoon's perspiration from his lightly freckled forehead with a red bandanna. He didn't tuck it deep into his jean's back pocket, but left out a red corner, at the ready for the first sign of an impending Happy Ram sneeze. Fair judges frowned on wearing animal fluids.

Brad looked his finest, and so did Happy Ram. After eliminating a dozen other county champions of various breeds, the judges awarded the pair the grand championship ribbon. Our family gathered around Brad and ram for newspaper and next year's fair program pictures. "Hold it, shhh, here comes the announcement," he urged, standing slightly straighter and taller than usual. We all stopped to listen for his name to ring out across the fair grounds.

"Congratulations to Ben Welton, owner of the Michigan State Fair grand champion ram," the mispronunciation echoed down the midway. His chance at fame gone, Brad deflated. He looked down and shook his head. Perhaps Happy took Brad's gesture as a queue, because the now nasally overcharged Happy Ram rotated his head to and fro, jettisoning a particularly massive white streak. We all jumped of its way, inspected each other, and then laughed at surviving a slippery close call.

Big Moo

Todd and his 4H project in 1959, a Hereford cow named Big Moo.

My oldest brother Todd started the family herd of white-faced Herefords toward the end of the 1950s. His favorite cow was a good-natured bovine he called Big Moo. She was his first show cow and won her share of blue ribbons at the county 4H fair. Big Moo was a beautiful red with a white face and neck line. Her offspring were also prize winners and she remained on the farm for many years.

Big Moo was friendly and cooperative, but often of a singular focus. If she wanted to go get a drink of water, no amount of pulling her lead rope changed her mind. Once she determined a patch of lush grass needed her attention, no fence could stop her. She was a hard keeper and a practiced escape artist. Her method of overcoming these barriers to greener pastures was slow and simple. The rotund beast sidled up to a taut woven wire fence, and then ever so slowly leaned into it. If she felt no electrical shock, she adjusted her rear end closer to freedom and against the metal fence post. Inevitably, the fence gave way. Then she carefully and delicately side stepped through and over it. Once clear, she turned and bee-lined to her destination.

While it was true that Big Moo could be stubborn and didn't always agree with the terms of a leash, Todd handled her with ease. He led her around the barnyard when he practiced his show ring technique and sometimes allowed one or two of us to ride on her broad back. Being submissive on a leash was important for showing and managing his cattle, so Todd trained calves when young and lightweight. Rebellious heifers were tied to a wooden fence post with an eight foot rope and then fed and watered for a few days so they could get used to the limitations of the lead line.

Steers had it tough from head to tail. When the time came, they were subjected to castration, and that was followed a few months later by the blood spurting procedure of having their horns removed.

Big Moo moved only after deliberation. Before expending energy, she looked about and contemplated her route with big brown eyes, accented with long white eyelashes. She had a sweet breath, a feminine look and the wiles to match.

One all night foray of freedom took her to a farmer's yard five miles away by breakfast. It was a long walk for Todd and Big Moo back to our farm, providing lots of time for Todd to enhance her leash manners.

Her consumption of hay and grain and subsequent discharge were the talk of many a county fair barn patrol volunteer. By the end of the fair week the long, white-washed wooden barns had roof high mounds of straw and manure at each end, waiting for tractors with front loaders or manure spreaders to recycle the organic accumulation. For years after her last 4H show, the call of "There's Big Moo's pile," rang from the back seat when our family drove by the empty fairgrounds.

Owning and showing a farm animal at the county fair made a youth eligible to stay overnight at the fairgrounds. As a twelve-year-old, bunking at the fair was the best part of the summer for me.

The farm girls were housed upstairs in the two-story wood-framed dormitory or bunkhouse. Meals were served on the first floor and only girls were allowed up the stairs. The boys had a circus sized tent to sleep in, and that suited me just fine.

Iron bed frames with mattresses that saw the light of day for only one week a year waited in rows under the dark green canvas tent. Since the county fair was in August, heat could beat down on the tent one day and rain the next.

With forty or so twelve- to seventeen-year-old boys, it didn't take much of an atmospheric change to set off their internal ballasts. Todd's distinctive tonal control and quantity were often the talk over breakfast.

In the humid semi-darkness of early morning, the night noises rose and waned around the tent. I had heard a similar rhythm and exchange of calls when camping by a lake with an active bull frog population. Some boys were most skilled in replicating the bawl of a lonely heifer. I was impressed by the concentration of talent and proud to be part of the farm boy fair fraternity.

Sleeping on an unfamiliar mattress, I wondered if I was the only one using it. A small squeak from underneath me drew my attention. I froze and waited silently to hear it again. There it was, a squeak for sure. I rolled onto my stomach and pressed my ear to the mattress. Eek, pause, eek, pause, eek. No doubt about it, something was there, and the little squeaks were coming faster. I was wide awake and expecting something to gnaw out of the cotton stuffed mattress and into my stomach. I could feel my heart pounding in fear. The squeaks came with every beat, and in a flash I realized it was the coiled springs squeaking with the pounding of my heart. What a relief. I relaxed after that self-inflicted close call and fell asleep to a rusty bedspring symphony of sympathetic squeaking.

FALL

Strange Animals

Unusual animals attracted plenty of attention on our farm, and many left lasting impressions. One crisp school day morning in late November my older sister, Patrice, came in from doing her morning chores. As she closed the door and looked back across the yard, she saw a red fox standing in the open and watching her. The fox was in the pasture near the gate.

"Hey, look at that fox!" she announced to the rest of us. My twin sister, Amy, and I looked at each other across the dinner table and raised our eyebrows. Our father was at the end of the table, having his coffee and listening to Bud Guest on WJR AM. He reached to the radio, turned down the volume and got up from his captain's chair that creaked loudly in the sudden silence.

"Let's take a look, have the dogs seen it?" he asked. The fox was only yards away from the dog pen that held two of his bird dogs. Our yard dogs, left unleashed, were curled up outside by the same door Patrice came in. They had followed her up to the house from the barn.

The pack was waiting to escort us to the end of the driveway when the bus arrived, part of their usual routine on school days.

Dad looked out and sure enough, a red fox was standing there, tail down and head held low, just below its shoulders. "That's not normal for a fox to do that," Dad observed. "Something's wrong with it."

Mom and the rest of us crowded behind Dad to see the critter. Being almost the end of deer season, it was not uncommon for a twelve gauge shotgun to be propped at the ready by the back door. The slugs were kept on a shelf above the nearby coat rack, the red, black and brass shotgun slugs in line like a row of soldiers awaiting orders. No sooner had he finished speaking when he grabbed two shells and loaded his Remington, closing the pump action with a fluid metallic "schlick." The dogs outside heard the familiar sound and jumped to their feet, looking up at us. Dad opened the door halfway, and then elbowed his way onto the porch, pulled up and without hesitation shot at the fox. The blast fractured the quiet chill of the morning and echoed back to us from the pole barn siding.

The dogs, who still hadn't seen the fox, started barking anxiously at the discharge. The two bird dogs, also baying, leapt about in their pen. The roar of the school bus downshifting for our stop added to the sudden eruption of noise. Dad held the door for us in one hand, and his shotgun in the other. We raced down the flagstone walk and looked back to see the fox, lying crumpled behind the fence.

After school I jumped off the bus and ran to where the fox had fallen, but it was gone. Dad had taken it away from all the other animals and buried it. He said the animal looked healthy but may have been infected with rabies. I walked off the distance, it was 85 yards, a shot worth bragging about, but Dad never mentioned it again.

Dad had a couple of encounters with flying squirrels in our farmhouse. One time, frustrated after his thwarted attempts to eradicate them using standard procedures, he loaded his double barrel twenty gauge and went after one in our only bathroom. The method proved effective, though the Christmas gifts hidden in a closet also suffered mortal wounds. After that showdown about five generations of flying squirrels returned on occasion to stage counter attacks. Once, Dad woke from a deep sleep to realize one wriggled under the covers with him. The squirrel escaped the ensuing thrashing, but managed to bite Dad deeply in the chest. A series of anti-rabies injections followed. They were so painful, Dad stopped after four of them. We had all read the book and seen the movie Old Yeller and were convinced we might have to chain Dad in the corncrib for two weeks to see if he developed symptoms of the foaming mouth delirium. An anxious few days passed until Dad declared himself in the clear.

A groundhog fell to the sword after being cornered on the front porch by one of our smaller dogs. The rodent was not taking the annoying yapping and snapping lightly. Dad, after judging that his pet was about to get a mauling by a groundhog, stepped back into the parlor of the house and grabbed the first weapon available, a WWII German blade in a ceremonial scabbard. A parry then a thrust, and the threat was kaput.

A large bird escorted me from the farm house to the woods a half mile away at the north end of the property. I was standing on the front porch, preparing to go for a hike and saw it walking up the driveway. I thought it was a guinea fowl, but the thing was almost as big as a hen turkey. I left the porch to investigate, and the bird disappeared into the weeds by the garage. Off I went on my walk. Twenty minutes later I was sitting at a favorite spot in the woods when I almost came out of my skin at a raucous crying from a tree thirty yards to the north. I may not be able to identify all the birds and animals that call the wild lands in the area, but I am familiar with them and this was something I had never heard on the farm before. In fact, I had heard it at a zoo. The cry of a peahen. Was she stalking me? That peahen must have been passing through because I never saw her again.

A number of animals remain mysteries. One I didn't see, but I felt it in the blackness of the night of my bedroom. It crossed my bed and legs, and in my semi-dream state, decided it must be a kitten and slipped back to sleep. The next morning, after a moment of clarity, I realized that we had no kittens, or even cats, currently extant in the house. My fear tempered somewhat as I recalled how each tentative step crossed my bedspread; it was for sure not a slither.

A UFO, or unidentified frying object, lit up my bedroom one warm fall evening. I had just clicked off my reading lamp and was settling in to sleep. Mom, Dad and my two sisters were watching TV downstairs. I had my window open and was lying on my back watching the single light bulb in the ceiling change shapes in the near darkness and listening to the night sounds of the farm. A noise I focused on was an irregular scritch, scritch. "That's claw on bark," I guessed, and judged the sound to come from just across the road.

One more scritch and my room lit up in a blue-white flash, followed by a crack like a rifle shot. A guttural cry and yowling that sounded eerily human went on in a rising pitch, then a vicious growling noise as it fought something. My body felt in a grip, my blood, cold milk from fear. "Ten, twelve, fourteen," I counted the seconds deliberately to control my fright. Darkness and quiet closed in. My fear-splashed mind felt sure that a beast was now climbing to my second story window. I beat a hasty exit down the stairs and to the dark living room and rest of the family.

"A raccoon must have climbed the utility pole and crossed the transformer wires," assessed Dad. We lit candles and waited for the power company to come restore the connection to our home. The men never found the 'coon.

"Could have been one of those flying monkeys from the Wizard of Oz," Amy argued, having recently watched the classic. For years after that, when crossing the road and passing the pole, I feared encountering a partly fried and angry chupacabra, its blackened skin shrunken on the skull, exposing sharp rows of teeth..

As a closing lesson to never eat food in the bedroom, I offer this equation. The formula goes something like this: eating food and not cleaning up equals crumbs that attract bugs and mice. Moving up the food chain, we find that bugs and mice are enjoyed by, among other predators, snakes. The resultant product over the years in our farmhouse was a well-fed three-foot-long milk snake that lived upstairs long after we emptied the nest.

To be fair to my siblings, recent onsite discoveries indicate the triggering food source not to be crumbs or leftovers, but dog food nuggets stashed away upstairs and nibbled on by not so unusual rodents.

Opening Day

When I was eleven years old, there were two nights of the year when I was too excited to sleep. Christmas Eve and the night before opening day of pheasant season, October 20.

My uncle and his two Brittany Spaniels never failed to arrive early in the morning before the season officially started. He bred and raised the dogs for field trials and Dad owned a couple because he thought they are naturally good bird dogs. The difference being that field trial dogs worked entire fields before a judge's stand, earning points for the number of pen raised pheasants or quail the dogs could locate and point within a set period of time. This kind of find'em fast hunting didn't work on our farm, as the birds were more likely to run than to hold tight.

The crunch of gravel as Uncle Herb pulled his station wagon into our driveway initiated a standard series of events in our yard. First, our family dogs surrounded his car and barked like mad at his caged spaniels. Second, Dad's Brittanys launched themselves up the wire fence of their pen and leap about hysterically at the sound of their two compatriots yapping in the car.

When my uncle let his two dogs jump over the tailgate of his car, they immediately attacked our farm dogs, snarling and fighting until he waded into the boiling pack and booted the dogs apart. The orange and white Brittanys righted themselves and made a beeline to their penned cousins. This caused the captive canines to escalate their greeting to near hydrophobic madness. The cacophony wasn't wasted on the skittish ringnecks that often fed in our garden.

Dad had to wedge his way past my uncle's dogs to open the pen gate. The four dogs exploded across our yard, raced through the garden and disappeared into the heavy swamp grass near the creek that bordered our property.

Birds, deer, rabbits and other game vaulted ahead of the hysterical dogs. The only time the purebreds slowed was to fight each other in a pitched gangland style encounter of growling and yelping. Hearing the melee, my brothers and I were sure they were killing each other.

"The dogs are just getting the kinks out," our watching uncle grunted over an unfiltered cigarette.

Viewing the roiling mayhem, my dad and uncle whistled and called out in vain, then elevate their enticings to a degree of foul-mouthed threats to the dogs and finally, they blamed each other for the dogs' disobedience. Then it was their turn to engage in loud and fierce exchanges.

The men obviously had years of practice at this and saved the most personal and threatening anatomical epithets for the final two or three minutes. My brothers and I regrouped near the barnyard, fearful of being caught in the vocal crossfire. We passed the time by looking over the pasture and marking where the escaping birds took refuge.

The words, coming faster, louder and hoarser were accentuated by one or more shotgun blasts into the morning sky in a final attempt to attract the bolting Brittanys back to the yard.

The season opened, as it does now, at 10 a.m., giving the birds a chance to move from their nighttime cover to water or into standing fields of corn. With an hour to go before legal shooting, we retired to the farmhouse for a breakfast of eggs, grits, bacon and coffee, even though the stimulant wasn't needed. We were all charged on adrenaline from the initial greetings.

I made a practice to collect the spent shells and sniff the intoxicating smell of burnt gunpowder, sometimes wearing them on my fingers at the table while listening to the retelling of last year's hunting successes and the achievements of my uncle's field trials.

The dogs, now muddy and loaded with burdocks, were brought inside to allow the 80 acres of the farm they had just stampeded through to cool down a bit. The wild-eyed dogs investigated the house and joined in cornering our placid housecat, terrified and looking down from the top of our bookcase in the parlor. Mom raised a concerned eyebrow as the mixture of man's best friend and house cat, swamp dirt, and various body temperature materials deposited onto our oriental rug. Looking back, it's a wonder she didn't make the first kill of the season right there in the house.

The old Seth Thomas wall clock chimed and the two men pushed away from the table, hooked their thumbs under their wide, red suspenders and declared it time to hunt some birds, the moment I had been waiting for.

I wasn't old enough to hunt with a shotgun, so I was issued an old bolt action army training rifle without the bolt. The rifle was as long as I was tall and weighed as much as one of the dogs. But I didn't complain. When we entered the field, I felt I was part of the brotherhood of hunters.

As the most junior, it was left to me to push through the tangled raspberry canes along the fencerows or flank the men as they hunted the corn field edges. I walked the corn fields, feeling the tug and gash of the rough-edged corn stalk leaves, trying to keep up with the jingle and tink of the Brittany's collar bells.

The men talked in low, gruff voices, "He's gettin' birdy," "Work'em over here," "Git in here, dammit," came the common refrains.

My two older brothers hunted with us, but often wandered into other fields when things were slow, hoping to bump up a rabbit. My uncle didn't like that. He claimed their diversions could cause his dogs to become nothing more than "bunny runners."

When the dog bells went silent, everyone stopped and located the one on point. Most of the time another dog checked up short of the one on point and also froze. "Look at Max honoring Snag's point," my uncle boasted as Dad and he closed in to flush the game.

The two men worked slowly to within a few feet of the dogs and stopped, holding their pump action twelve gauges at the ready. After hearing us trudging nearby, this silence was powerful pressure on wild game. After a few tense seconds, a bird erupted straight up for a few feet, then leveled off and gained airspeed with every wing beat. Everyone reacted by snapping their shotguns to their shoulders and drawing down on the bird.

"Hen!" someone shouted needlessly. The bird continued to rocket away for a quarter mile before briefly setting her wings and angling into heavy cover to land.

I felt the rush of excitement spike and then wane within a few seconds, my face cooling. The dogs buried their noses in the birds hiding spot and their stubby tails wiggled. Their earlier misbehavior was forgiven and praise lavished on them.

It took two days of morning and afternoon hunting to cover the sweet spots on our farm and by then the dogs had settled down and were working close, retrieving the occasional ringneck pheasant.

The men and their dogs grew old together in the fields and are all long gone now. The dog pen and graves of Dad's Brittanys are overgrown with scrub brush and weeds. But a connection still remains. I no longer carry that old rifle, but use a field worn double barrel my dad hunted with for forty years. The farm is still in the family and on opening day the fall colors, the smell of heather and a flushing bird from a familiar fence line still elicit that gloriously alive feeling.

Small Game Hunting

With a supply of corn and oats that ran into the tons, it was no wonder that growing populations of rats and mice claimed the old tin roofed carriage barn on our farm as their own. When they crossed the line by threatening our animals, it was left to me to settle things.

The barn served as a garage, horse tack area, corncrib and oat bin. With such a food supply, the hordes of rats grew fearless and many were seen in daylight. The recalcitrant beasts often gathered beneath a canvas tarpaulin on the floor of the horse tack area. I made it a point to flip the sheet and watch the rats leap in all directions at least once a week. They streaked away to hide underneath the nearest object in seconds. I sometimes managed to stomp a boot onto a slower rodent.

At other times I might catch one and toss the captive into an empty five gallon paint bucket. It was safer to have only one in the bucket. I had tried two and they attacked each other in their panic, then both boiled out of the bucket. I dumped the bucket in the yard and soaked the rat with a stream of water from the garden hose as it hopped and ran toward the nearest cover, our birddogs' pen. The two excited Brittanys tried to chew through the wire fence when the escaping rats scooted along the outside edge to disappear in the weeds.

This entertainment evolved when my neighbor Larry and I started using BB guns on the fleeing vermin. We could always count on two or three rats to hop and run from under the tarp, offering a quick shot. We missed our fair share and had rats run over our feet to get away.

Our brigade of barn cats had fought the rats to an equilibrium of sorts. The antagonists kept a distance from each other. One August afternoon, I watched our old, tough female cat we called Starlight stagger out of the garage onto the gravel driveway, head shaking in bursts, both ears torn and patches of skin show-ing from her plucked fur coat. The rats had fought her off as she tried an ambush and she had suffered a beating. I figured ol' Starlight was down to two or three of her original nine lives.

Then our smallest and sweetest dog came out the worse from a tangle with a mob of barn rats, and we declared war. I gained parental clearance for mop up operations in the carriage barn. I was almost thirteen and pretty handy with my lever action Ithaca single shot twenty gauge. My first field of fire was the far end of the corncrib. The grey or brown rats worked beneath the boards of the almost empty crib and often crept up the wall boards thirty feet away to the eve. This location offered the best shot, before they scampered along the eve to the oat bin. The heavy boards easily stopped my scattershot. I had to be careful not to shoot the metal roof.

Sitting in the corncrib in the evening with just minutes of shooting light left, I planned my last shot of the day. I heard scratching and muffled squeaks beneath the wooden Vernors ginger ale box I used as a seat. I caught sight of shadows drifting beneath the crib's shrunken floorboards. The rats had a system that let two rats use the same runway in different directions. When one rat met another, the dominant rat crawled over the other and continued on his way before the other started up again. I remained still, sitting at the ready in the corncrib, rats only inches away beneath the worn boards.

The brass bead on my barrel wasn't that easy to see in the fading light, but I drew down on a rat, covered the moving shadow and blasted away. The orange-yellow flash from my shotgun filled the corncrib. The roar echoed for miles into the evening. The farm fell silent, then thumping hoofbeats rang out as our horses spooked and galloped across the pasture.

After a few ear ringing nights, I decided the better location was on the roof peak over the corncrib.

Following a day of eating grain, the rats loped from the crib beneath me, across the barnyard to the new pole barn that had fresh hay and a water supply. The shooting was good under the blue-green light of the mercury pole lamp halfway between my perch and the new barn. Dust flared like flames into the night air around my quarry with every discharge. In my mind, the rajahs in India never had it as good from their elephant top tiger hunting.

The rest of the family was safely in the farmhouse, enjoying some prime-time TV as I waged my pesticide. I passed the time composing in my head a rat hunting story for Outdoor Life or Field and Stream magazines. Nifty nuggets recycled from other adventure stories made their way into my mental draft. "It was an unguided hunt in untapped territory," "The game was at a peak of their population cycle and I was the first white man to witness the herds," or "I hunted the great browns, the famed Norway rats." I offered tips, best shotgun round, when to hunt, and how to spot a trophy rat (females were the biggest). A rat coming my way became a charging menace that I had to miraculously stop with my last bullet in the last sentence. In a more lucid moment, I realized those magazines may not consider it in their best interests to promote night hunting of rats from rooftops.

I was able to catch a number of pigeons on the same peak with my bare hands. For some reason, the birds roosted there at night and did not flush with my approach. I could crab-walk on my fingers and tennis shoe toes up the shadowed side of the gently pitched metal roofing right up to the birds. After gathering one under my shirt, I slid down the roof and jumped from the eve seven feet to the ground. My sisters were waiting by the barnyard light pole to see if I really could catch a bird bare-handed. I was happy to show off my climbing and stalking skills. The girls inspected the bird for lice, gave it a name and let it go. We watched the rock dove flap out of the light into the blackness as I scratched my chest and wondered.

Overhead in September

A few weeks after the start of school, blackbirds start to fly overhead in ever growing numbers, a sure sign that fall is just a cold wind away in Michigan. One Saturday, of my early ninth grade, Larry and I were riding our bikes to town in search of candy and classmates.

Directly above us a flock of chattering red winged blackbirds flitted southbound in a narrow, barrel-like formation that undulated across the cool blue sky, furling with the wind. We stopped at our intersection to see just how big a flock it was. It stretched as far as we could see. We mounted our bikes to ride south with the birds.

It was always a gamble to ride into town with no money, hoping to collect enough roadside empties to stake us to a pop and candy bar. I needed six empty pop bottles to have enough for a Mallo Cup candy bar and a Coke. The milk chocolate cup was packaged with collectible coins printed on a cardboard square. I planned to save up the required 500 "cents" to mail away for a free box of ten.

We were always on the lookout for bottles, dead bugs and road kill mammals. A sighting stimulated a change in conversation. "See those coons up there," nodded Larry from his bike as he coasted and banked into a corner ahead of me. A sun swollen coon and three smaller ones came into view. I coasted for a better look.

"The mamma got hit and her babies stayed by and got runover, too," he relayed from beyond the site of the massacre.

The bottle deposit was two cents, and we saved the money for treats at our one-stop-light village. It was a small town, less than a thousand homes in the entire school district. But it supported four grocery stores and four full service gas stations. This was before gas stations started selling bread and milk but focused on the traveling man's necessities that included tobacco, oil, cigarettes and newspapers.

On hot days, a good choice for a cold pop was the widow Bradshaw's small grocery store. The distinguished white-haired lady offered ice cold pop from a water-filled chiller near the manual cash register. Twelve ounce bottles stood in lines of flavors suspended from long metal tracks, keeping only the caps above the circulating ice cold water. On a scorcher of a day, it was always a treat to hold the bottle and most of my forearm under the water until the cold almost hurt.

Mrs. Bradshaw gave us credit for a small bag of potato chips and pop when our gleaning came up shy. Mom settled the bill during the next day's visit.

Pickings were good on that three mile ride into town. Larry and I uncapped our colas, using the bottle opener and bucket attached near the countertop cash register. Our poptops chattered like poker chips into the tin. The two drinks cost a nickel each and with the deposit, came to fourteen cents. Larry and I sat on the curb in the shade by our bikes and savored our chocolates, chugged our cokes, and claimed our four cent deposit. My toe flicked back the kickstand of my bike and I swung my leg over to mount up and cruise the sidewalks and alleys of our hometown.

We pedaled around and explored what was new. Part of the day trip included stopping at the ball field for a long drink from the always on water fountain. To pass the time, Larry and I practiced squirting streams of water between our teeth or reading tracks left in the dusty ground around the fountain and the ball field. Tire tracks from cars and trucks could elicit a long, creative interpretation of how many girls were riding, their hair color, how fast the car was moving and the song being played on the radio, a remarkable feat of deduction and exaggeration from fellow hunter and tracker Larry.

After a moment's study of the infield's flat and dusty ground, Larry offered an opinion over the bas relief chain-link design of bicycle tracks, dog and cat pug marks. A mosaic track made by Converse All Stars high tops was common. Not quite the variety of spoor seen around the watering holes of the Serengeti Plains of Africa, but interesting enough to us thirteen year olds.

The September sun was setting a pumpkin orange, throwing our shadows across the village street as we headed home on our bikes. Walking toward us was a group of four upperclassmen. A dirt clod burst on the pavement nearby, so Larry and I zigged and zagged down the middle of the street. The sissy-armed boys pretended to throw rocks our way after missing us by a mile. They bragged that they were going up the water tower as we passed on the far side of the roadway.

I looked at Larry who met my glance and shook his head. Climbing the water tower was the crown jewel of delinquent acts in our hometown. To climb to the see-through wire circular catwalk, up ten more feet along the tower's reservoir, backwards over the roof's edge and then onto the ladder up the smooth steel of the conical roof was bravery and stupidity unquestioned. On Monday mornings in high school, before first hour, the largest crowds around any school locker were at the feet of these legendary daredevils as they retold of their weekend victory over the constant tug of gravity and authority.

For others, leaving their mark was sometimes needed to validate water tower claims. It didn't take much of a handwriting expert to name the vandal who used a paint roller to write his initials on the tank. Authorities made sure the common-sense-challenged climber never made it to school for his well-deserved Monday brag.

The day's light was slipping away when the two of us raced and coasted our bikes toward home. From a half mile away, we saw the dark cloud of blackbirds high over the crossroad. The flock went from northern to southern horizon in the changing blue sky. This long, fingerlike flock had been flying overhead all afternoon. How many blackbirds? Larry and I couldn't think of a number big enough. "What's after a billion?" we asked each other while staring up at the chattering birds.

"I don't know," I dreamed out loud, "but I'd love to have that much Mallo Cup money."

School Day Mornings

A family's preparation for the first day of the school year has changed significantly since I was an elementary school student in the 1960s. Today, mobile phones, backpacks, shoes that cost more than my first term in college and looking good for a fresh profile picture on FaceBook are new considerations. For the current generation when school resumes, the little scholars summer rhythm of late nights and sleeping past noon may take days of languid adjustment compared to a single terse warning that if ignored, was followed by a long walk to school "back in the day."

By the time my dear twin sister and I were entering kindergarten our mom had developed a streamlined and efficient system for launching her five children into the world of higher education. All of us in a varying yet structured order, woke, dressed, looked for the other sock, vied for time in the lone bathroom, did morning chores, put together a lunch, eat and left the house in time to catch the bus. When behind schedule, we could save a moment by leaping over the hedge around our front porch and gain speed down our hill frantically skidding to a halt at the end of the driveway. Brakes screeched and hissed as the bus stopped just short of our pack of yapping dogs. For our lunches, preparation began in early August. Mom kept a sharp eye for bread to go on sale. When the price was right, she filled her shopping cart with twenty or thirty loaves. She then finagled a discount on twenty or more pounds of sliced pickle loaf lunch meat.

Soon after, rows and columns of white bread slices covered our dinner table. An assembly line of kids took up stations. My older sister Patrice squirted her initials in mustard on alternating pieces and Mom dealt a slice of lunch meat onto the others. Amy and I followed them around the table, flipping the slices together and sometimes adding an unwatched glob of butter or extras salt and pepper.

After thousands of sandwiches, Mom gained the practiced motion of a casino card dealer. She easily shuffled over 200 sandwiches together, stuffed each into a clear plastic fold and seal bag, stacked them in the original bread bags, and pack them into the deep freeze. When the time came, she grabbed one or two and dropped them along with an apple into a brown lunch sack or tin lunch box. By noon, these original fast-food sandwiches thawed into a sustaining, if somewhat slimy and freezer-burned, substance.   130

The ice-locked hoard of nutrition was finally exhausted in 2008 when the freezer coughed and expired. Emptying it felt like evaluating a time capsule. Layers of food-like objects revealed an evolution in packaging and changing tastes of our great nation. Beneath shriveled and crystalline wild game, livers, cow tongues, ox-tails and multicolored garden vegetables resided the bottom layer, the final repository of a lonely and forlorn sandwich that had last seen the light of day during President Kennedy's administration.

The school day started for me when I heard my brothers clumping down the stairs an hour before the bus arrived. They had to feed and water their animals, change out of their barn clothes, eat breakfast and catch the bus. When the backdoor rattled closed, I'd snuggle back under my blanket and be thankful I wasn't raising any sheep or steers. Having witnessed the relentless day after day animal husbandry demands, I had negotiated my daily chores of feeding the dogs and taking out the trash to an after school schedule. I was conscripted into helping my siblings only due to illness or threat of bodily harm.

My oldest brother Todd even checked his trap line for muskrat and mink during cold and bleak winter school days. The hunter-gatherer could have been on that US Army recruiting poster claiming a day's work done before breakfast.

My sisters crawled out of bed before me to allow time for changing wardrobe choices and hair styles (not as complicated as today's girly procedures requiring lip gloss, hair gel, eye lash underlining, highlighting, hair blow drying and the application of mineral powders, metallic pins, rings, studs and other facial hardware).

The first kid to finish his cereal was assigned as lookout for the bus. After reading Herman Melville's Moby Dick, my second oldest brother, Brad, became convinced "Thar she blows!" was an appropriate call to action when the lumbering school bus was spotted. From our hilltop farmhouse, he could spy the bus coming down the grade a half-mile away, allowing a good forty seconds to grab our coats and blast out the door.

Mom sent each of her five kids out the open door with a generic "dear" and a word of encouragement, unable to match names with faces as she had yet to have her second cup of Maxwell House coffee. Or was it multi-child stress syndrome? Ask any multi-child mom for more details. I have been known to call out my

dog's name by mistake when addressing offspring at risk of injury or mayhem.

Most kids who take the bus to school
know that their education begins on the morning ride and ends in the afternoon when the
folding doors of the bus close behind them.

After saying good morning to our
beloved driver, my sisters and I plopped onto
our seats and looked about quietly. Physical
activity and foul language were kept to a minimum by the ever watchful eye in the wide mir-
ror on the bus driver's window visor. The latest
news of bizarre animal behavior or family con-
flict spread from seat to seat as fast as the
erupting malignant odors issued from milk and
sugar charged passengers. The latter met with
responses ranging from tearful looks of shame
to triumphant boasting.

My fellow riders often debated if our
driver had the same gift as our school's librari-
an to move both eyes independently or did she
have an extra ocular manifestation beneath her
hair on the back of her head? Whatever the
case, her talent in quelling juvenile behavior
before thought became action was indisputable
and well known.

It was a great morning when a substi-
tute driver piloted our orange monster to town

and school. When that happened, a small rodeo often broke out for the twenty minute ride. In that respect, things haven't changed much after all.

WINTER

Lady and the Sleigh

Most of the animals on our farm were registered stock. Although the bloodlines were pure, the animal's disposition was often up for question. Purebred animals could go off the deep end more easily than mixed breeds, it seemed. Sometimes I knew what caused the breakdown, sometimes I didn't.

It was pretty easy to figure out what triggered a wild reaction of a horse one November weekend years ago. Lady was the oldest and most docile horse on the farm. She was a tall, fat Tennessee Walker mare and had lived on the farm for years. She was the first horse my twin sister rode.

At the age of three, Amy had taught herself to shinny up the left front leg of the gentle horse and climb onto her back, ready to ride. Our older sister Patrice first rode a pony, and then quickly moved on to showing horses. The two sisters could manage any horse on the farm by the time they were twelve and nine years of age, respectively.

I had just knocked an arm long icicle from the garage roof and was looking through it at the low white sun in the overcast sky. Amy trotted up. "Patrice wants you to get the old sleigh out, so Lady can take us for a ride," she relayed. We weren't surprised that Patrice made plans for a holiday drive using the ancient sleigh stored under tarpaulins in our garage/corncrib. She'd mentioned to us something about sledding through the pasture after gazing at an antique winter scene print hanging in the farmhouse parlor.

A light dusting of snow the night before added a clean freshness to the gritty snow in the pasture. It had been two weeks since the last snowfall on the opening day of deer season. The girls gave up horseback riding around the farm during the two week whitetail gun season. Patrice tried riding with all red coveralls and a hand written cardboard sign saying HORSE that hung across the saddle, but felt staying around the barn for a couple of weeks the more prudent decision. The decision gave her time for other equine projects such as having Lady hitched to the old sleigh.

I was drafted into moving the almost forgotten sleigh out of the back of the garage and up the hill by the house. After cleaning out the burlap bags, empty pop bottles, oil cans and other filler, the sleigh didn't look half bad. The single seat sat crookedly on a wooden frame painted black and trimmed with pin lines of red. The box was mounted on a pair of sleigh runners made of wood and iron. The front of the sleigh curved up and over, just like the old Currier and Ives prints.

The antique black sleigh still had the long curved shafts, but no harness. "We'll just use some baler twine," Patrice decided, "like we did to make the reins longer.".

Amy finished unraveling some twine and knotted a make-shift harness. She and Patrice then went to get Lady. The old hayburner was standing in her usual spot beside the corncrib, waiting patiently for a chance to eat all the corn she could. The girls cajoled Lady into a bridle, and the old horse sauntered behind them as they came up from the barnyard to the staging area under the oak trees in our yard. Amy was leading Lady, holding both reins, and the two stopped by the newly fashioned harness. Lady exhaled a long steamy breath in the chill afternoon air. She seemed almost bored, though tolerant.

Patrice led the mare around the sleigh to familiarize her with it. The horse held her nose to the black horse hair seat and her eyes opened wider. "Once she knows what's behind her, she won't bolt away like Midget did," Patrice said.

She was recalling a botched experiment when we tied a red Radio Flyer wagon to our Shetland pony. As usual, I was assigned the test pilot seat. The plan was for me to get into the wagon and have Amy lead Midget around, pulling me merrily along. The mean little pony was off at a gallop as soon as Patrice finished double knotting the baler twine harness to him.

It was amazing how strong the twine was. The scared pony ran in a panic as the red wagon dragged, skipped and flew in the air behind him. After a quarter mile dash, the wagon caught on a scrub tree and mercifully broke free of the near hysterical pony. "I think next time, we'll use one of our teddy bears as a test pilot," I had reflected as Midget stared back at us, his ribcage heaving.

Once Patrice felt confident that Lady was comfortable with the odd looking sleigh, she and Amy set about attaching the harness. The old mare tossed her head up and down and looked back at me. She didn't look so sleepy-eyed now. In fact, she appeared wide awake, and her hooves fidgeted nervously on the frozen ground. I was given the honor of hold-ing the reins until my sisters could board the sleigh and take over the controls.

"After a practice ride around the barn-yard, we will be all set to give Mom and Dad a ride later today," Amy predicted, as she hopped into the sleigh next to me. Lady shifted her weight to the side Patrice was working on and turned her head to look at us, her eyes showing more white than usual. Though I was no horse-man, I suspected that when a horse was wide-eyed, there were only moments left to calm the animal before panic set in.

Seeing that Lady was showing more concern than usual, Patrice quickly finished another double knot and jumped in with Amy and me. Lady turned her head forward and dug in, her haunches dropping to secure more pur-chase. She lunged forward. The slack snapped out of the twine harness.

The sleigh jolted ahead, causing a reac-tion untempered by the earlier desensitizing walk around. Lady snorted and bolted into high gear. A Tennessee walking horse has many gaits, from a slow walk to a quick stepping fast walk. None of us had ever seen her run, but now we had a great view. Clumps of packed snow and sod from her galloping hooves went flying over our heads.

The sleigh, unevenly attached to the power source, was gaining speed and skewing to one side, just missing Lady's rear hooves as it angled away from behind her. We covered twenty or so yards, then the sleigh banged into an oak tree. Amy and I somersaulted from the seat onto the frozen yard.(As luck would have it Amy cushioned my fall, a timely and wel-comed coincidence. She claimed I pushed her, of course.)

We stared at our older sister, now riding solo. The old mare was grunting and throwing her head up and down as she put her weight into her fight or flight reaction. Fortunately, the girls had left the gate to the barnyard open and Lady made a bee-line for it. The sleigh tipped onto its side causing Patrice to hastily give up the reins and tumble to a stop.

Lady ran like the wind after the sleigh broke free, her long black mane, golden baler twine and upheld tail furling behind her.
"So much for giving Mom and Dad a ride down a snow covered lane," Patrice said, turning the sleigh upright.

"Yeah, well, maybe we can tie the toboggan to Lady and give them a nice sled ride," Amy suggested. We had done it before with a Christmas tree on the toboggan but another horse had done the pulling.

"If they want to stay on longer than you and I did, we'll have to tie them in," I laughed.

January Sail Skating

Growing up, winter sports for me included outdoor ice skating, a term that could mean a number of related contests. Take sail-skating as an example.

The fastest I ever went on skates had to be when I used my winter coat as a sail and rode a southerly breeze across a wind swept lake.

A January warm front was pushing across the farm from the south after a week of low teen temperatures that had limited my amount of time outside. I was a thirteen year old with cabin fever that I am sure was contracted from my two sisters who always seemed to be up to something.

I had hopes for glass smooth ice and little snow on the small lake on our property. The gusty winds and moments of bright sunshine made for a great day to spend outside and skate.

I dug up a long winter coat, stocking cap and mittens and stomped into my boots, leaving the farmhouse with my skates tied and draped around my neck. I unleashed Snoopy, my black and white beagle, and we headed to the north end of our eighty-acre farm, a half mile trek through pastureland and woods. The top branches clacked and crashed against other tree tops. "It certainly is windy!" I observed to Snoopy, who happily looked up at me, his tongue flopping out one side of his mouth.

The lake surface was a mixture of various sized rough white ice patches on a smooth as glass surface. Jets of white shot clear ice that had fractured during expansion. The ice reflected the high rippled clouds and clear blue of the sky. I sat on my mittens and changed into my skates, judging the temperature to have climbed out of the twenties..

I skated away, getting the feel of the ice, into unblocked wind. Loyal Snoopy stayed behind in the thick cattails that partially sheltered him from the winter blasts. He poked around at promising clumps of reeds or swamp grass and cast an occasional glance my way as he worked the frozen shoreline.

I turned my back to the gusting wind, unzipped my coat, put my hands in the pockets and held my arms outstretched. (I've seen this design recently in those bat wing suits worn by nuts that jump off windy canyon cliffs and sail around.)

I gathered speed, then coasted, and then picked up speed again with every blast. Try as I might, I could not find a direct unblocked route from south to north shore, but did have some long runs and set many world speed records that day. Slowing down became a choice among turning sharply and making crystal rooster tails, plowing into crusty snow-covered ice, or falling down, with the latter often in conjunction with the former.

A Close Shave

A dry, chill early December wind was finally blowing away a lingering fall in the mid-1960s. Dad was in the lone bathroom of our 1880s farmhouse, enjoying a leisurely shave late on a Sunday morning. He had lathered his face with shaving soap whipped into a foam with a badger hair brush in a small wooden bowl. His "T" shaped razor held a fresh double-edged stainless steel disposable razor blade. I was first in line to use the bathroom and was leaning against the door frame, passing the time watching him shave as I had many times before. Dad made a pig-like face when he took a finger and pushed his nose to one side. He oinked at me and with a deft double down stroke shaved his upper lip, then wiped the remaining dot or two of foam from his face. To finish, Dad splashed warm water onto his face and then patted dry with a linen surgical towel salvaged from some routine operation on the farm. Thick napped bath towels were few and far between, but he had a good supply of old towels recycled from his medical office. To top it off, he sprinkled drops of Vitalis on his hands and ran his fingers through his hair

Holiday season was in full swing and fancy foods were in season. Stuffed dates rolled in powdered sugar tempted us from the marble topped table in the parlor. A coffin-sized cardboard box sent from Florida arrived with oranges and grapefruit, compliments of the village pharmacy. In the living room, the hardwood nut bowl bulged with filberts, home grown walnuts and hickory nuts. Silver dishes with redskin peanuts and cashews beckoned. The cashews were carefully rationed with each refilling, and were always picked out and eaten first.

Everyone in the family grazed on treats from one area of the house to another. This included our Siamese cat apparently, as the stuffed fig dish was usually empty in the morning. This hadn't gone unnoticed by Dad. "I'd guess the cat is climbing the Christmas tree,"he postulated. "Then he's jumping over to the table and eating them."

Our expecting Siamese cat had gone missing days before, so my sisters and I knew she must have had her kittens. Not that she was missed that much. The cat was given to us by someone who claimed the animal had cabin fever and needed a larger place to call home. She wasn't a friendly cat and like most cats, had her quirks and other mental issues. Now it

appeared as if like she were coming out of hiding at night to raid the holiday food.
Apparently her special canned cat food wasn't good enough for her.

As noisy as the house was during the season, my dear twin sister Amy had heard a soft, familiar mew coming from an overstuffed upstairs closet. Kittens were in there all right, confirmed our older and wiser sister, Patrice.

This kind of news demanded action. I ran into the backyard with my cornet and started blowing.short staccato notes. The honking brass was one of many ways to communicate with my best friend and neighbor, Larry, half a mile away across open field and lowlands. Soon I heard the plaintive bleating of his cornet in response. I gave a few more urgent blasts and waited, looking his way. Larry appeared at the road intersection moments later, pedaling and coasting on his bike to our house.

"What's the big deal?" Larry asked as he tipped his bike over and came in the back door. "Our Siamese cat had kittens. Let's go see'em," I reported. Amy, Larry and I crept up the stairs. The closet opened off the upstairs hallway and was big enough to have its own door. Old coats and jackets that we were expected to grow into hung patiently. Paper grocery sacks and large cardboard boxes full of

147

clothes covered the floor space. With no light, we agreed it was an inviting location for a cat to have kittens.

The three of us approached with caution as we knew from experience that a new animal mother is defensive and dangerous. A growl came from six feet deep in the darkness. It trailed off into silence.

"Maybe we should come back in a couple of days," Amy suggested over my shoulder as we peered into the closet.

At the sound of her voice, the cat hissed and jumped into the light, halfway to the doorway. She gave us a squinty, red-eyed stare, and backed into the shadows, growling. The false charge scared us, so we turned and ran for the stairway. But apparently our retreat was not enough appeasement for the momcat. She began wailing louder, and then jumped out of the closet shadows onto the hallway rug. Then she bolted down the hallway after us.

In fearful haste Larry and Amy were skipping two or three steps down the narrow stairway, close behind me. The cat leapt between two spindles of the banister and onto Larry's head. Before he could scream in reaction, the cat jumped down onto Amy's head, gathered her feet beneath her and launched from my twin's carrot-top onto my noggin and into space. Her trajectory landed her on the living room floor with a thump. The feline's four clawed feet dug into the carpet. She shot across the living room, under the dining room table and into the back room, going full tilt and headed for the refuge of the basement. Then she crashed into the closed basement door and dropped over.

The three of us milled about in a tangle at the foot of the stairs. We were holding our heads, looking for blood and simultaneously describing the animal attack we had just survived.

Dad stood up from the table in the dining room and approached the basement door. After a moment, he declared her expired. "She was a sick cat," he opined. "I'm not sure what was wrong with her, maybe a brain parasite made her crazy."

"Could we catch it from her?" I asked, rubbing my scalp with newfound concern. My older sister Patrice stepped from the parlor. "You probably gave it to her," she said, her fingernails clawing at an orange to mock me.

We gathered around the cat's limp body. Upon closer inspection she didn't look very healthy. We chose cremation instead of burying her alongside our other, more loved, pets.

The cat left behind two kittens that we raised on the bottle until they were old enough to give away. We didn't want to take a chance that the kittens were infected or WOULD grow up to be as mean as their mother.

As an unsuspecting, kind-hearted lady was taking the last one to her car, she paused and told us that Siamese cats were kept in Asian temples for protection.

"The cats instinctively jump on the heads of intruders," she said. "If you look at an ancient Chinese soldier's armor, you can see chain mail hanging from their helmets, protecting the back of their necks from claws and fangs. Can you imagine a cat on your head, scratching away?" she asked.

Amy raised her eyebrows and fixed her eyes on me. "Oh, wow, that's scary," she said innocently.

The Miserable Little Christmas Tree

Reprinted from a family newsletter sent to friends in December, 1968

.

by Willah Weddon

It wasn't too soon before Christmas, and it wasn't too late. It was just the right time to bring home a Christmas tree. Father stopped at the town square to pick one out for Patrice, Amy and Alex. He carefully inspected each tree. There were half-a-hundred of them, all laid in rows, and they were all very little. It took a long time to pick one.

Finally, he found one that was the tallest of them all, although it was as round as it was tall and thick as a bush. Paying the man in charge four dollars, Father put the little tree in the trunk of his new 1965 Buick Riviera and drove home. The children gathered around as he pulled the tree out and stood it up. It was shorter than the smallest child. There were needles all over the inside of the trunk.

"We'll put it in a bucket of water and let it soak," Father said. "Then the needles will stop falling."

"And maybe it will grow," Alex said hopefully.

They tried to sweep the needles out of the trunk with a whisk broom. They stuck very tight to the upholstery, and when they came loose, the needles jabbed the children's fingers. Father got one under his fingernail.

"These are miserable little needles," he determined. Then he had to saw a piece off the bottom of the tree and trimmed a few lower branches so it fit into the water bucket. The tree sat in the water, behind the house for a week. Each night, when the children got off the school bus, they inspected it. The needles continued to drop.

"It's getting shorter," Alex wailed.

"I don't think it wants to be our Christmas tree," Patrice said thoughtfully.

"It's a miserable little tree," Amy confirmed.

Mother tried to console them. "It will be nice when we get it in the front room."

"But we've always had a big, beautiful one," Patrice insisted. "We've got to do something."

Saturday Father announced, "Tomorrow we will put up the tree."

The children looked at each other and

nodded their heads. They had thought of something.

Early in the morning, Patrice said she was going for a ride on her horse, Amidore. Alex agreed to go with her. It was cold and blowing. There was snow on the ground. Amidore pawed with her front hooves. She did not like the steel bit in her mouth. They did not put a saddle on her because they were going to ride double. Alex crawled up behind Patrice. The warmth of the animal felt welcome in the cold.

Lad, the Collie, and Snoopy, the hound, followed along behind as they headed north into the fields toward the woods. As they road by a swale, two reddish-brown deer bounded out with their white tails waving like flags. As they leapt away, Snoopy bayed.

Father bundled up and went out to put the little tree in the standard, so he could bring it into the house. It did not quite fit. He had to saw off more branches. When it finally went in, it skewed stubbornly to one side. He had to saw off a little more from the base. Still crooked. His hands grew cold. The stubs on the unyielding tree scraped and scratched his fingers.

Father let out a yell. "Where are the children? They've always helped before."

Inside the house, Mother shook her head

sadly. "We've always had such a happy time putting up the decorations. This miserable little tree is making our Christmas miserable too." She put the potatoes in the oven with the chicken and decided to bake a cake. A treat to make everyone feel better.

Suddenly Amy called down from upstairs. "Look out the window. Here they come."

Alex was dragging a beautiful blue spruce behind him. Snoopy followed. Patrice came along leading Amidore. Lad trailed them all.

"See what we found, Dad," they called out. "One of our own."

Father looked up. He'd planted some pine trees a few years ago, way back by the woods. They had started to grow. But one long, cold winter the deer had nibbled the tops. Everyone thought they had killed the baby trees. He'd forgotten about them.

Patrice had seen some growing when she had been out riding last summer. Remembering this, she'd told Alex, and they'd decided to go and see how big the trees had become. Alex had taken his Boy Scout hatchet along, just in case.

This was a beautiful tree. Father smiled. Then he grabbed what was left of the little tree he had been trimming and sawing and shortening. He tossed it far over the eastern downhill slope of our hilltop back yard we called "The bank." The overgrown area of scrub brush and noxious weeds was the repository of all that was deemed useless. The brittle collection of needles made a nasty sound as it landed.

After dinner the family decorated their new tree. Pine sap oozed from the tips of the branches and filled the rooms with the smell. Perfectly shaped, it reached nearly to the ceiling of the parlor. They put the star on top and admired it while enjoying chocolate cake and vanilla ice cream.

"It's our own tree too," Father said with pleasure. "grown on our own farm."

"There are more, not as large, but they will grow." Patrice and Alex told him. "This one seemed just right for us."

"Thank goodness we don't have to put up with that miserable little tree." Amy sighed.

"Shhh," Father warned her. "That little bush might hear you, come back over the bank, and counter-attack."

Everyone laughed. It was a merry, merry Christmas after all.

The end
Close Calls of the Farm:Second Chances

Samples from the table of contents:
Close Calls on the Farm:
Survival of the Funniest

Close Calls on the Farm:
Off to School

www.CloseCallsOnTheFarm.com
for ordering information.